MRT-DOF

W9-AHM-175

DÉPÔT
DEPOSIT

THE AMSTERDAM TREATY

A comprehensive guide

OBN 1604198

This booklet is published in all the official EU languages of the European Union: Danish, Dutch, English, Finnish, French, German, Greek, Italian, Portuguese, Spanish and Swedish

This document is also available on the SCADplus internet site: http://europa.eu.int/scadplus/

A great deal of additional information on the European Union is available on the Internet. It can be accessed through the Europa server (http://europa.eu.int).

European Commission
Directorate-General for Education and Culture
Publications Unit, rue de la Loi/Wetstraat 200, B-1049 Brussels

Cataloguing data can be found at the end of this publication.

Luxembourg: Office for Official Publications of the European Communities, 1999

ISBN 92-828-7951-8

ZZ
EM410
99A57

© European Communities, 1999
Reproduction is authorised provided the source is acknowledged.

Printed in Germany

PRINTED ON WHITE CHLORINE-FREE PAPER

CONTENTS

INTRODUCTION

Background

The Amsterdam Treaty, agreed by the European Union's political leaders on 17 June and signed on 2 October 1997, is the culmination of two years of discussion and negotiation in a conference of Member State government representatives. It has now entered into force after being ratified by the 15 Member States of the European Union under their respective constitutional procedures.

Former Article N of the Treaty on European Union specifically required an intergovernmental conference to be convened to review certain provisions. In the first half of 1995 each of the Community institutions prepared a report on the functioning of the EU Treaty. A reflection group chaired by Carlos Westendorp, the Spanish Secretary of State for European Affairs, then devoted the second half of the year to an in-depth analysis of the possible options. The group presented its report to the Madrid European Council in December 1995.

After consulting the Commission and the European Parliament, whose opinions had to be obtained before the intergovernmental conference could be launched, the Turin European Council formally opened the negotiations on 29 March 1996. They included a number of ambitious goals centred on a Citizens' Europe, the role of the European Union on the international stage, improvements in the working of the institutions, and the prospect of enlargement.

A series of European Councils in Florence (21 to 22 June 1996) and Dublin (twice — 5 October and 13 to 14 December 1996), and an informal Council in Noordwijk (23 May 1997) scrutinised and discussed the various proposals. After 15 months of work, a consensus emerged on the Amsterdam Treaty.

Objectives of the Amsterdam Treaty

The aim of the negotiations was clear: to create the political and institutional conditions to enable the European Union to meet the challenges of the future such as the rapid evolution of the international situation, the globalisation of the economy and its impact on jobs, the fight against terrorism, international crime and drug trafficking, ecological problems and threats to public health.

The mandate of the Intergovernmental Conference was partly determined by the treaties themselves, but the European Council added a number of specific questions about the working of the institutions, such as the composition of the Commission and the weighting of votes in the Council. Other subjects raised by the Community institutions or the Member States were also added to the agenda as the negotiations progressed.

Structure of the Treaty

The Amsterdam Treaty consists of three parts, an annex and 13 protocols. The Intergovernmental Conference also adopted 51 declarations, which are annexed to the Final Act. It also noted a further eight declarations by various Member States, which were also annexed to the Final Act.

The first part covers the substantive amendments and comprises five articles:

- Article 1, which contains the amendments made to the Treaty on European Union;
- Article 2, which contains the amendments to the Treaty establishing the European Community;
- Article 3, which contains the amendments to the Treaty establishing the European Coal and Steel Community;
- Article 4, which contains the amendments to the Treaty establishing the European Atomic Energy Community;
- Article 5, which contains the amendments to the Act annexed to the Council Decision of 20 September 1976 on the election of representatives to the European Parliament by direct universal suffrage.

The second part of the Treaty — Articles 6 to 11 — deals with the simplification of the treaties establishing the three European Communities and their annexes and protocols, with a view to deleting lapsed clauses and adapting the text of certain provisions accordingly (Articles 6, 7 and 8).

It also provides for the repeal of the Convention of 25 March 1957 on certain institutions common to the European Communities and the merger Treaty of 8 April 1965 (Article 9). However, it makes clear that this simplification exercise does not alter the legal effects of the texts or the acts in force adopted on the basis of them (Article 10). The Court of Justice is competent to interpret the provisions of this part of the Treaty (Article 11).

The third part — Articles 12 to 15 — contains the general and final provisions of the Treaty. Article 12 relates to the renumbering of the provisions of the Treaty on European Union and the Treaty establishing the European Community, Article 13 specifies that the Treaty is concluded for an unlimited period, Article 14 deals with ratification and entry into force, and Article 15 lists the different language versions.

The annex to the Treaty contains the tables of equivalence for the renumbering of provisions of the Treaty on European Union and the Treaty establishing the European Community. There are 13 protocols:

- Protocol on Article 17 (ex Article J.7) of the EU Treaty, dealing with the western European Union and the progressive framing of a common defence policy;
- Protocol integrating the Schengen *acquis* into the framework of the European Union;
- Protocol on the application of certain aspects of Article 14 (ex Article 7a) of the Treaty establishing the European Community to the United Kingdom and to Ireland;
- Protocol on the position of the United Kingdom and Ireland in relation to the new Title of the Treaty establishing the European Community on 'visas, asylum, immigration and other policies related to free movement of persons';
- Protocol on the position of Denmark in relation to the new Title of the Treaty establishing the European Community on 'visas, asylum, immigration and

other policies related to free movement of persons' and to certain aspects of the common foreign and security policy;

- Protocol on asylum for nationals of Member States of the European Union;
- Protocol on the application of the principles of subsidiarity and proportionality;
- Protocol on external relations of the Member States with regard to the crossing of external borders;
- Protocol on the system of public broadcasting in the Member States;
- Protocol on protection and welfare of animals;
- Protocol on the institutions with the prospect of enlargement;
- Protocol on the location of the seats of the institutions and of certain bodies and departments of the European Communities and of Europol;
- Protocol on the role of national Parliaments in the European Union.

What the Treaty accomplishes

This guide is primarily concerned with the amendments made to the Treaty on European Union (EU Treaty) and the Treaty establishing the European Community (EC Treaty). For the sake of clarity, it has been divided into four major chapters dealing with the main reforms introduced by the Treaty of Amsterdam.

Freedom, security and justice

This section explains the guarantees introduced by the Amsterdam Treaty to protect fundamental rights within the European Union, such as equality between men and women, non-discrimination and data privacy.

It also discusses the changes concerning freedom of movement within the European Union and the inclusion in the EC Treaty of a new title on visas, asylum, immigration and other policies linked to the free movement of persons.

The section concludes with an outline of the new Title VI of the Treaty on European Union, which deals with police and judicial cooperation in criminal matters and the conditions for the integration of the Schengen *acquis* into the legal framework of the European Union.

The Union and the citizen

This section consists of seven fact sheets setting out the improvements brought in by the Amsterdam Treaty in areas directly affecting the rights, interests, and well-being of individual citizens. The major changes are:

- the development of the concept of European citizenship, with additions to the list of civic rights enjoyed by citizens of the Union and a clarification of the link between national citizenship and European citizenship;
- the insertion into the Treaty establishing the European Community of a chapter on employment, providing for the development of common strategies for employment and the coordination of national policies;
- the incorporation into the Treaty establishing the European Community of a stronger social agreement with a commitment to tackle social exclusion and uphold equality between men and women;
- the consolidation of environmental policy, with emphasis being placed on sus-

tainable development, the consideration of environmental aspects in all sectoral policies and the simplification of Community decision-making;

- an improvement in the instruments available to the European Union for promoting high standards of public health;
- the clarification of the aims of consumer protection policy and better integration of the measures taken in this area with other policies;
- a guaranteed right of access for each citizen to the documents produced by the European Union institutions and the right to communicate with the institutions in their own language. Emphasis is placed on improving the standard of drafting to make legislation easier to understand and apply.

Effective and coherent external policy

This chapter sets out to describe the improvements made by the Treaty of Amsterdam to enable the European Union to defend its interests more effectively on the international stage.

It consists of two sections, an economic one dealing with extending the scope of the common commercial policy, and a political one on the reform of the common foreign and security policy (CFSP).

The economic section elucidates the challenges and practicalities of extending the scope of the common commercial policy to include international agreements on services and intellectual property rights. The section on the CFSP looks at the following reforms:

- the creation of a new instrument: the common strategy;
- improved decision-making thanks to greater use of qualified majority voting in the Council;
- the creation of the post of High Representative for the common foreign and security policy to give the CFSP greater prominence and coherence;
- the establishment of a policy planning and early warning unit to encourage joint analysis of international developments and their consequences;
- the incorporation of the 'Petersberg tasks' into Title V (CFSP) of the Treaty on European Union, to demonstrate the Member States' common desire to safeguard security in Europe through operations to provide humanitarian aid and restore peace;
- the simplification of the procedures for funding the CFSP.

Institutional questions

This section summarises and explains the institutional reforms envisaged by the Amsterdam Treaty with a view to the enlargement of the European Union. Clarification is provided on several points:

- the scope and operation of the co-decision procedure, strengthening the role of the European Parliament;
- the weighting of votes in the Council of the European Union and the extension of qualified majority voting;
- the structure and operation of the European Commission, particularly the number of Commissioners, the Commission's power of initiative and the role of the Commission president;
- the role of the Court of Justice in areas such as fundamental rights and certain matters closely affecting the internal security of the European Union;

- an enhanced role for the Court of Auditors, the Economic and Social Committee and the Committee of the Regions;
- greater involvement of national parliaments in the activities of the European Union and better provision of information for them;
- consolidation of the subsidiarity principle by the inclusion of a protocol containing legally binding guidelines;
- the possibility of closer cooperation between those Member States who want it.

These reforms constitute a first step. A general revision of the institutional arrangements in the treaties will be the subject of another intergovernmental conference to be convened before membership of the European Union exceeds 20.

FREEDOM, SECURITY AND JUSTICE

Fundamental rights and non-discrimination

Introduction

The founding Treaties contained no specific provisions on fundamental rights. The credit for gradually developing a system of guarantees for fundamental rights throughout the European Union has to go to the Court of Justice.

The rulings given by the Court have been essentially based on:

- Article 220 (ex Article 164) of the EC Treaty establishing the European Community, which requires the Court to ensure that the law is observed in the interpretation and application of the Treaty;
- the political dimension of the Community, which is grounded in a European model of society, including the protection of fundamental rights recognised by all Member States.

By bringing fundamental rights to the fore, those who drafted the Treaty of Amsterdam were endeavouring to give formal recognition to human rights. The provisions of the new Treaty include the following:

- Article 6 (ex Article F) of the EU Treaty has been amended so as to reaffirm the principle of respect for human rights and fundamental freedoms;
- a procedure is laid down for dealing with cases where a Member State has committed a breach of the principles on which the Union is based;
- more effective action is to be taken to combat not only discrimination based on nationality but also discrimination based on sex, racial or ethnic origin, religion or belief, disability, age or sexual orientation;
- new provisions on equal treatment for men and women are inserted in the Treaty establishing the European Community;
- individuals are afforded greater protection with regard to the processing and free movement of personal data;
- the Final Act was accompanied by declarations on the abolition of the death penalty, respect for the status of churches and philosophical or non-confessional organisations, and on the needs of persons with a disability.

Background

The place given to fundamental rights in the Community Treaties has changed considerably since the European venture was first launched. At the outset, fundamental rights were not a central concern of those who drafted the Paris and Rome Treaties, which reflect a sectoral and functionalist approach. The Treaty of Paris, which established the European Coal and Steel Community

(ECSC), is concerned solely with the coal and steel industries. This sectoral approach gained strength after the failure, in 1954, of the European Defence Community (EDC) and the concomitant moves towards political union. It thus became a feature of the Rome Treaties establishing the European Atomic Energy Community (Euratom) and the European Economic Community (EEC). Although the EEC Treaty was wider in scope than the other two, all three Treaties covered well-defined economic spheres.

One consequence of this sectoral approach was to set the founding Treaties apart from any basic law of a constitutional nature which incorporated a solemn declaration on fundamental rights. The Treaties in question were not suited to the inclusion of such a preamble, particularly since the Council of Europe's European Convention on Human Rights (ECHR), signed in 1950, already provided an advanced model for the protection of human rights in Europe.

The situation changed rapidly as the Court of Justice, in the judgments it handed down, began to monitor the respect shown for fundamental rights by the Community institutions and the Member States whenever they took action within the areas covered by Community law. The Court recognised, for example, the right to property and the freedom to engage in economic activity, which are essential to the smooth operation of the internal market. The Court held that fundamental rights ranked as general principles of Community law and that they were based on:

- the constitutional traditions of the Member States;
- the international Treaties to which the Member States belonged (and the ECHR in particular).

In 1977 the European Parliament, the Commission and the Council signed a joint declaration in which they undertook to continue respecting the fundamental rights arising from the two sources identified by the Court. In 1986 a further step was taken when the preamble to the Single European Act included a reference to the promotion of democracy on the basis of fundamental rights.

The EU Treaty states that 'the Union shall respect fundamental rights, as guaranteed by the European Convention for the Protection of Human Rights and Fundamental Freedoms signed in Rome on 4 November 1950 and as they result from the constitutional traditions common to the Member States, as general principles of Community law' (Article 6(2), ex Article F.2).

At the same time, the idea that the Community as such should accede to the ECHR had begun to circulate. The Council decided to ask the Court's opinion on whether membership of the Convention would be compatible with the Treaties.

In its opinion of 28 March 1996 the Court held that, as Community law stood at that time, the Community was not competent to accede to the Convention.

As European integration has progressed, the European Union has gradually widened its field of action, reflecting the determination of the Member States to act as one in areas which until now have been a strictly national preserve (e.g. internal security or the fight against racism and xenophobia).

In view of these changes, which necessarily go beyond the sectoral context of the Community's early days and impinge on the daily life of European citizens, there is a need for clear legal texts which proclaim respect for fundamental rights as a basic principle of the European Union. The Treaty of Amsterdam meets this need.

Principles

The Treaty of Amsterdam clarifies Article 6 (ex Article F) of the Treaty on European Union (which will become Article 6 once renumbered as provided by the Treaty of Amsterdam) by stating unequivocally that the Union is founded on the principles of liberty, democracy, respect for human rights and fundamental freedoms, and the rule of law, principles which are common to the Member States.

It also amends the preamble to the EU Treaty, confirming the Member States' attachment to fundamental social rights as defined in the European Social Charter of 1961 and the Community Charter of the Fundamental Social Rights of Workers of 1989.

Before the Treaty of Amsterdam entered into force, Article F.2 of the EU Treaty stressed respect for the rights guaranteed by the ECHR and those resulting from the constitutional traditions common to the Member States. However, under former Article L (now renumbered Article 46) the powers of the Court of Justice did not extend to Article F, so limiting its impact. Since ensuring respect for the law in the interpretation and application of the Treaty is the Court's task, the scope of fundamental rights was correspondingly reduced.

By amending Article 46, the Treaty of Amsterdam ensures that Article 6(2) will be applied. The Court now has the power to decide whether the institutions have failed to respect fundamental rights.

Breach by a Member State of the principles on which the Union is based

The Treaty of Amsterdam proclaims that the Union is founded on the principles of liberty, democracy, respect for human rights and fundamental freedoms, and the rule of law, principles which are common to the Member States. At the same time, the new Treaty acknowledges that these principles may be infringed by a Member State and lays down the procedure which the Union should follow in dealing with the Member State concerned.

Establishment of the existence of a breach

On a proposal from the Commission or one third of the Member States, the Council — in the shape of the Heads of State or Government — may determine the existence of a breach by a Member State. The breach must be 'serious and persistent'.

The European Parliament has to give its assent by a majority of its members and a two-thirds majority of the votes cast. The government of the Member State in question is first invited to submit its observations.

The Council's decision establishing a breach will be considered unanimous even where a Member State abstains.

Suspension of the Member State concerned

Once a serious and persistent breach has been established, the Council may (but need not necessarily) suspend some of the Member State's rights under the Treaty. However, the country remains bound by its obligations. The suspension of rights might, for instance, involve withdrawing the Member State's voting rights in the Council.

At this second stage, the Council acts by a qualified majority, disregarding the votes of the Member State concerned.

Variation or revocation of the suspension

If there is a change in the situation that led to a Member State's suspension, the Council can decide to vary or revoke the measures taken.

When taking such a decision, the Council acts by a qualified majority, disregarding the votes of the Member State concerned.

The fight against discrimination

Article 12 (ex Article 6) of the EC Treaty provides that any discrimination on the grounds of nationality is prohibited. At the same time, Article 141 (ex Article 119) lays down the principle of non-discrimination between men and women, though only as far as equal pay is concerned.

The Treaty of Amsterdam restates the principle of non-discrimination in stronger terms, adding two new provisions to the EC Treaty.

The new Article 13

This Article complements Article 12, which prohibits discrimination on grounds of nationality. The new Article enables the Council to take appropriate action to combat discrimination based on sex, racial or ethnic origin, religion or belief, disability, age or sexual orientation.

When the Council acts on the basis of Article 13, it does so unanimously on a proposal from the Commission and after consulting the European Parliament.

Declaration regarding persons with a disability

The new Article 13 provides for measures to combat discrimination based on disability. The Intergovernmental Conference that drew up the Treaty of Amsterdam sought to offer an even stronger guarantee by including a declaration in the Final Act, stating that the Community institutions must take account of the needs of persons with a disability when adopting measures to approximate Member States' legislation.

Equality between men and women

Article 2 of the Treaty provides that it will be the Community's task to promote the harmonious, balanced and sustainable development of economic activities, environment-friendly growth, a high degree of convergence of economic performance, a high level of employment and social protection, the raising of the standard of living and quality of life, economic and social cohesion and solidarity among Member States.

Article 3 lists the various measures which the Community should take to carry out the tasks specified in Article 2.

The Treaty of Amsterdam extends these two Articles to include equality between men and women, which previously figured only in Article 141 (ex Article 119) of the EC Treaty (more restricted in scope since it relates only to equal pay). The two additions made are as follows:

Amendment of Article 2

The list of tasks facing the Commission will include the promotion of equality between men and women.

Amendment of Article 3

A new paragraph has been added, reading as follows:

'In all the other activities referred to in this Article, the Community shall aim to eliminate inequalities, and to promote equality, between men and women.'

Processing of personal data

The main Community measure in this area is the 1995 directive on the protection of individuals with regard to the processing of personal data and on the free movement of such data.

In the absence of a specific legal basis, this directive was adopted under Article 95 (ex Article 100a) of the EC Treaty, which concerns the approximation of legislation relating to the single market.

The free movement of persons necessarily entails the establishment of information systems on a European scale. In view of these changes, a new article has been inserted in the EC Treaty, making the rules on the protection of individuals applicable to the Community institutions themselves.

The new Article 286

This Article will consist of two paragraphs which will provide respectively that:

- from 1 January 1999, Community acts on the protection of individuals with regard to the processing of personal data and the free movement of such data apply to the Community institutions and bodies;
- before 1 January 1999, the Council is to establish an independent supervisory body responsible for monitoring the application of those Community acts to Community institutions and bodies.

FREEDOM, SECURITY AND JUSTICE

The gradual establishment of an area of freedom, security and justice

Introduction

For more than 20 years now the Member States have joined forces to combat international phenomena such as terrorism, drug trafficking or illegal immigration. By 1986, however, when freedom of movement for people was recognised as a key element of the internal market, it was clear that this type of informal cooperation between the Member States' governments was no longer adequate to combat the international spread of crime networks or satisfy the public's need for security in Europe. It was therefore decided to incorporate cooperation on justice and home affairs into the Maastricht Treaty so as to make it a fully-fledged policy of the European Union.

An intergovernmental pillar has been grafted onto the Community pillar and legal instruments of a new kind have been created. Cooperation on these lines was set up following the entry into force of the Treaty on European Union in 1993 but has not been seen as very satisfactory in terms either of how it works or of the results it has produced. So the revision of the EU Treaty has brought in some major changes in the decision-making process.

To create an area for freedom, security and justice, the Treaty of Amsterdam will introduce a new title headed 'Visas, asylum, immigration and other policies related to free movement of persons' into the Treaty establishing the European Community. Controls on external borders, asylum, immigration and judicial cooperation on civil matters all now come under the first pillar and are governed by the Community method. The incorporation of these areas into the Community, however, will be a gradual process dictated by the speed at which the Council of the European Union takes the decisions, to be completed by the latest five years after the entry into force of the new treaty. Only police and judicial cooperation in criminal matters remains under the third pillar, to which the new Treaty adds preventing and combating of racism and xenophobia.

These institutional developments bring in new types of decision taking, which should make it possible to adopt more — and more effective — measures, leading to closer cooperation between Member States.

Historical background

The beginnings of cooperation (1975–85)

From 1975 onwards intergovernmental cooperation was gradually established in the fields of immigration, the right of asylum and police and judicial cooperation. The first instance of this was the Trevi Group, in which the Ministers for Home Affairs met for the purpose of combating terrorism and coordinating police cooperation on terrorism in the Community. The Ministers in the Group discussed questions relating to law and order and terrorism, and various working parties and subparties were set up under its auspices. The European institutions were at the time excluded from this process, which was conducted on an intergovernmental basis.

From the Single Act to the Treaty of Maastricht (1986–92)

The Single European Act concluded in 1986 was a turning point in this process of cooperation, which up until that point had functioned in a far from transparent way as regards the public and the Community institutions. A new Article 8a defines the free movement of persons as one of the four main constituent elements of the single market and explicitly brings that field within the Community's sphere of jurisdiction. The new working parties set up after the signing of the Single Act took account of this development and from that point on included observers from the Commission. In addition, the *ad hoc* working party on immigration, which has since 1986 consisted of the ministers responsible for immigration, and CELAD, the European Committee to Combat Drugs, set up their secretariats with the secretariat of the Council of the European Union. Other working parties were set up, such as the Mutual Assistance Group or GAM, which is responsible for customs matters. A Council consisting of the Member States' Ministers of Justice used to hold regular meetings. From that time onwards it used to deal with judicial cooperation in criminal and civil matters and certain questions falling within the sphere of European political cooperation.

Despite the recommendations on free movement of persons in the Commission's White Paper of 1985, justice and home affairs continued to be largely matters for intergovernmental cooperation. In 1988, for example, the intergovernmental coordinators' group on the free movement of persons was instructed by the Rhodes European Council to propose measures for linking the free movement of persons and security together once controls at the internal borders had been abolished. In 1989 this group put forward a proposal for a work programme (the Palma document) advocating a more coordinated approach to the different aspects of cooperation on justice and home affairs. The fact was that the various working parties set up over the years were working separately and drafting their reports for ministers sitting in different combinations. What is more, the European Parliament and the national parliaments were unable to exercise any control over the measures taken in that context, owing to the very nature of the cooperation itself.

The instruments used were those appropriate to a traditional intergovernmental approach: on the one hand, conventions, and, on the other, the drawing up of resolutions, conclusions and recommendations. These acts, the classic instruments of international law, were adopted outside the Council of the European Union. They include the 1990 Dublin Convention determining the State responsible for examining applications for asylum lodged in one of the Member States of the European Communities, and the London resolutions also relating to asylum.

Instruments of a more binding type were adopted by some other Member States during the 1980s. These were the 1985 Schengen Agreement and the 1990 Schengen implementing convention, which set up new operational structures to ensure cooperation between police forces and customs authorities (through the Schengen Information System, SIS). It then became clear that the far from open system of consultation groups needed to be incorporated into a comprehensive structure: not only to make sure that the measures adopted by the Member States in relation to justice and home affairs were more effective but also to coordinate the work of all these bodies and avoid duplication.

Institutionalising cooperation in the fields of justice and home affairs: Title VI of the Treaty on European Union (1992–98)

Title VI was partly modelled on this pre-existing intergovernmental cooperation system, which explains the charges levelled against it that there were too many working levels within the third pillar and that it was over-complicated and not transparent enough. The way the third pillar was structured, on the lines of the common foreign and security policy, gave the Community institutions only a small part to play and no real way of exercising any control over the Member States' decisions:

- the Court of Justice was competent to interpret conventions only where there is a clause in the text (convention or other) expressly providing for this;
- the European Parliament could be consulted by the Council, but most of the time it was only informed;
- the European Commission's right of initiative was limited to certain areas and was shared with the Member States;
- the Council was often paralysed by the requirement to take every decision by unanimous vote.

The Treaty of Amsterdam has reshaped cooperation on justice and home affairs by setting up an area of freedom, security and justice. The aspirations are wider and more specific and the methods more effective and democratic, while the institutions have been given a more balanced role to play.

How Title IV of the EC Treaty works

Title IV encompasses the following areas:

- free movement of persons;
- checks at external borders;
- asylum, immigration and protection for the rights of nationals of non-member countries;
- judicial cooperation in criminal matters.

These are defined as questions of common interest and previously came under the rules laid down in Title VI of the EU Treaty (commonly known as the third pillar).

Establishing an area of freedom, security and justice in five years

The Treaty of Amsterdam has transferred these areas to the EC Treaty, where the role of the institutions is very different from the role they used to play under Title VI.

The Council of the European Union will continue to play the main role over the next five years so that it can take a number of decisions in the areas referred to above.

The object is to make it easier for European citizens and nationals of non-member countries to move freely, while at the same time building up effective cooperation between the different government departments concerned in order to combat international crime.

The overall institutional machinery

The Council is still the lynchpin of the process but it is no longer the only actor involved.

Over the first five years after the new treaty has come into force, the Council will take decisions unanimously on proposals put forward by the Commission or a Member State. It has to consult the European Parliament before taking any decision.

After that time, the Council will take decisions only on proposals from the Commission. The Commission, however, will have to consider any request by a Member State for a proposal to be put before the Council. After consulting the European Parliament, the Council will have to decide by unanimous vote to apply the co-decision procedure and qualified majority voting when adopting measures under Title IV and to modify the clauses relating to the Court of Justice of the European Communities.

Apart from its decision-making role, the Council's role as a coordinator between the relevant government departments in the Member States and between them and the European Commission has been consolidated. The many different levels of working party that currently exist have been abolished. All the working parties now stand on the same footing and report directly to Coreper (Committee of Permanent Representatives).

Some measures, however, come under a different institutional mechanism (Article 67).

The Court of Justice of the European Communities

The new Treaty gives the Court of Justice a larger role to play in the areas of justice and home affairs. Previously it had no powers in these areas and could not review the measures adopted by the Council. Only in the case of conventions did the Court have the right to interpret their provisions and rule on any dispute over their implementation — and even this only applied if they contained a special clause to that effect.

In the new Title IV, which essentially concerns free movement of persons, asylum, immigration and judicial cooperation in civil matters, the Court of Justice now has jurisdiction in the following circumstances:

- if a national court of final appeal requires a decision by the Court of Justice in order to be able to give its judgment, it may ask the Court to rule on a question concerning the interpretation of the title or on the validity and interpretation of acts by the Community institutions that are based on it;
- similarly, the Council, the Commission, or a Member State can ask the Court to rule on a question regarding the interpretation of the new title or of acts adopted on the basis of it.

The Court of Justice does not, however, have the right to rule on measures or decisions taken to abolish all checks on individuals (both EU citizens and non-EU nationals) when they cross internal borders.

The Member States

The Member States retain their prerogatives, above all as regards the free movement of persons. They continue to have sole responsibility for ensuring law and order and safeguarding internal security. In this context, they may take foreign policy considerations into account.

In the event of an emergency, if there is a sudden influx of nationals of non-member countries into a Member State, temporary measures (for a maximum of six months) may be taken by the Council voting by qualified majority on a Commission proposal in the interests of the Member State concerned with a view to restricting the freedom of movement or entry of the nationals of the non-member country concerned.

The protocols

1. Protocol on the position of the United Kingdom and Ireland

These two countries are not taking part in measures under Title IV and are not bound by them. They do not, therefore, take part in votes in areas falling within the area of security, freedom and justice.

If, however, the United Kingdom or Ireland wishes to take part in the adoption and implementation of a proposed measure, they will have to inform the President of the Council within a period of three months starting from the submission to the Council of the proposal or initiative. They will also be entitled to agree to the measure at any time after its adoption by the Council.

2. Protocol on the application of certain aspects of Article 14 (ex Article 7a) of the EC Treaty to the United Kingdom and to Ireland

The United Kingdom and Ireland reserve the right to exercise controls at their frontiers on persons seeking to enter their territory, in particular citizens of States which are contracting parties to the Agreement on the European Economic Area or to any agreement by which the United Kingdom and/or Ireland is bound, and the right to decide whether or not to let them enter their territory. At the same time, the other Member States may exercise controls on all persons coming from the United Kingdom or Ireland.

Ireland has expressed its wish to take part as far as possible in measures adopted under Title IV insofar as they allow the common travel area with the United Kingdom to be maintained. The common travel area is an area of freedom of movement between Ireland and the United Kingdom.

3. Protocol on the position of Denmark

Denmark is not taking part in measures under Title IV except those determining the non-member countries whose nationals must have a visa when crossing the external borders of the Member States and measures introducing a uniform format for visas.

As far as building upon the Schengen *acquis* is concerned, Denmark will decide whether to implement any decision in its national law within six months after the Council has adopted it.

How Title VI of the EU Treaty works

The object of Title VI ('Provisions on police and judicial cooperation in criminal matters') is to prevent and combat the following:

- racism and xenophobia;
- terrorism;
- trafficking in persons and offences against children;
- drug trafficking;
- arms trafficking;
- corruption and fraud.

These objectives will be achieved through:

- closer cooperation between police forces, customs authorities and other competent authorities in the Member States, both directly and through Europol;

- closer cooperation between judicial and other competent authorities of the Member States, both directly and through Europol;
- approximation, where necessary, of rules on criminal matters in the Member States.

Clearly, then, the objectives of Title VI of the EU Treaty have been made more specific. Aware that crime extends beyond national borders, the Member States have recognised that the only effective way to fight the international networks that have formed is through closer cooperation.

The overall institutional machinery

The Council of the European Union remains the main actor in the decision-making process under Title VI. To achieve the objectives set out above, it can use the following instruments:

- joint positions defining the approach of the Union to a particular matter;
- framework decisions to approximate the laws and regulations of the Member States. Like directives (the instruments used in the Community pillar), framework decisions are binding upon the Member States as to the result to be achieved but leave the choice of form and methods to the national authorities;
- decisions for any other purpose except approximating the laws and regulations of the Member States. These decisions are binding and the Council, acting by a qualified majority, adopts the measures necessary to implement them at Union level;
- conventions, which are adopted by the Member States in accordance with their respective constitutional requirements. Unless they provide otherwise, conventions enter into force once they have been ratified by at least half of the Member States that adopt them.

A coordinating committee consisting of senior officials draws up opinions for the Council and helps prepare the ground for its deliberations.

The Commission is fully involved in the discussions in the areas covered by Title VI and its power of initiative has been extended to cover all fields.

The Member States

The new Treaty does not affect the Member States' exercise of their responsibilities for maintaining law and order and safeguarding internal security.

The Member States have virtually sole responsibility for cooperation in the fields covered by Title VI. To coordinate their action, they inform and consult one another and establish collaboration between their respective government departments.

They uphold common positions adopted under this heading in the international organisations and conferences that they take part in.

The Member States may establish closer cooperation using the EU institutions, procedures and mechanisms. However, this must not encroach on the powers and objectives of the European Community and must be aimed at enabling the Union to develop more rapidly into an area of freedom, security and justice (as the Schengen system succeeded in doing earlier). The Council gives its authorisation by a qualified majority (a vote in favour by at least 10 members). If such closer cooperation creates problems for a particular Member State for reasons of national policy, the Council may ask for the matter to be referred to the European Council.

The European Parliament

Before adopting a framework decision or decision or establishing a convention, the Council has to consult the European Parliament.

The Presidency and the Commission will regularly inform the European Parliament of discussions in the areas covered by Title VI.

The European Parliament may ask questions of the Council or make recommendations to it. Each year it will hold a debate on the progress made in the areas of police and judicial cooperation in criminal matters.

The Court of Justice

The new Treaty recognises that the Court of Justice has jurisdiction to give preliminary rulings on the validity and interpretation of framework decisions and decisions, on the interpretation of conventions and on the validity and interpretation of the measures implementing them.

Regarding preliminary rulings, the Member States are required to make individual declarations accepting the jurisdiction of the Court of Justice and stating which national court or tribunal is empowered to request the Court of Justice for a ruling.

Depending on the Member State's choice, either the national court of final appeal or any court in the country may then ask the Court of Justice for a ruling on any question regarding the interpretation or validity of one of the above acts, if it considers such a ruling necessary to enable it to give judgment.

The Protocols

1. Protocol integrating the Schengen *acquis* into the framework of the European Union

The Member States that have signed up to the Schengen Agreements (all the Member States apart from the United Kingdom and Ireland) now conduct their cooperation on abolishing internal borders under the institutional and legal framework of the European Union. The Council has taken the place of the Executive Committee established by the Schengen Agreements.

Ireland and the United Kingdom may take part in some or all of the arrangements under the Schengen *acquis* after a unanimous vote in the Council by the 13 participating Member States plus the representative of the government of the State concerned.

Iceland and Norway are associated with the implementation of the Schengen *acquis* and its further development.

2. Protocol annexed to the Treaty establishing the European Community on asylum for nations of the Member States of the European Union

Since all the Member States of the European Union already respect human rights and fundamental freedoms, an application for asylum by a national of a Member State may be taken into consideration only in the following cases:

- if the Member State of which the applicant is a national takes measures derogating from its obligations under the Convention for the Protection of Human Rights and Fundamental Freedoms;
- if the Council has determined that there has been a serious violation of human rights in the country of the applicant;

- if a Member State should so decide unilaterally (Belgium has undertaken to give individual consideration to any application for asylum in order to comply with its earlier international obligations: the 1951 Geneva Convention and the 1967 New York Protocol).

Crossing internal and external borders

The Council of the European Union, within a period of five years from the entry into force of the Treaty, must adopt the measures necessary to attain the objectives set by the Treaty of Amsterdam.

Checks on persons at the internal borders of the European Union

All checks on persons, whether citizens of the Union or nationals of non-member countries, at the internal borders of the Union are to end.

In contrast to the other areas covered by Title IV, the Court of Justice does not have jurisdiction to pronounce on the validity and implementation of measures in this area.

Crossing the external borders of the European Union

The Council lays down the standards and procedures to be followed by Member States in carrying out checks on persons at the external borders of the European Union.

Common rules on visas for intended stays of up to three months include the following:

- a list of non-member countries whose nationals must be in possession of visas when crossing the external borders and those whose nationals are exempt from that requirement;
- the procedures and conditions for issuing visas by Member States;
- a uniform format for visas (Member States will issue the same format of visa to nationals of non-member countries);
- rules on a uniform visa (the issuing of visas by the Member States is governed by common rules).

The general procedure for decisions under Title IV requires measures under the second and fourth points above to be taken by the Council acting unanimously. Within five years after the new Treaty has come into force, such measures will have to be taken by co-decision with the European Parliament.

By way of an exception to the general procedure applied under this Title, measures under the first and third points above are decided by the Council by a qualified majority, acting on a proposal from the Commission after consulting the European Parliament.

Free movement of nationals of non-member countries

Measures will have to be adopted setting out the conditions under which nationals of non-member countries will have the freedom to travel within the territory of the Member States during a period of no more than three months.

Protocol on external relations of the Member States with regard to the crossing of external borders

The Member States retain the right to conclude agreements with non-member countries as long as they do not conflict with Community law and other relevant international agreements.

Asylum and immigration policies

Within five years after the Treaty of Amsterdam has come into force, the Council has to adopt measures in various areas relating to asylum and immigration. This time limit does not, however, apply to measures on ensuring a balance between Member States in accommodating refugees and displaced persons, on the conditions of entry and residence for immigrants, and on the rights of nationals of non-member countries.

Asylum policy

International rules on asylum were laid down by the Geneva Convention of 1951 and the New York Protocol of 1967 on the status of refugees. In addition, there will be consultations with the United Nations High Commission for Refugees and other relevant international organisations on questions of asylum policy. Against this background, the Council takes decisions to determine:

- the criteria and mechanisms for determining which Member State is responsible for considering an application for asylum submitted by a national of a non-member country in one of the Member States;
- minimum standards on the reception of asylum-seekers in the Member States;
- minimum standards with respect to the qualification of nationals of non-member countries as refugees;
- minimum standards on procedures in Member States for granting or withdrawing refugee status.

Other measures on refugees and displaced persons that also have to be adopted are:

- minimum standards for giving temporary protection to displaced persons from non-member countries who cannot return to their country of origin and for persons who otherwise need international protection;
- promoting a balance of efforts between Member States in receiving and bearing the consequences of receiving refugees and displaced persons (the problem of refugees from former Yugoslavia in Germany, in particular, has shown how useful such a measure would be if such a situation were to arise again).

In the event of one or more Member States being confronted with an emergency situation characterised by a sudden inflow of nationals of non-member countries, the Council may, acting by qualified majority on a proposal from the Commission, adopt provisional measures of a duration not exceeding six months.

Immigration policy

For this policy, measures will be adopted in the following areas:

- conditions of entry and residence, and standards on procedures for the issue by Member States of long-term visas and residence permits, including those for the purpose of family reunion;
- illegal immigration and illegal residence, including repatriation of illegal residents.

Measures will also be adopted defining the rights and conditions under which nationals of non-member countries who are legally resident in a Member State may reside in another Member State.

The Member States may maintain or introduce national provisions under their immigration policies as long as they are compatible with the Treaty of Amsterdam and with international agreements.

Judicial cooperation in civil matters

Since judicial cooperation in civil matters has cross-border implications, measures in this area are adopted under the arrangements of Title IV of the EC Treaty. The aims are as follows:

- assisting other Member States in understanding judicial and extra-judicial acts adopted in a particular Member State; improving and simplifying cooperation in the taking of evidence and the recognition and enforcement of decisions in civil and commercial cases, including decisions in extra-judicial cases;
- promoting the compatibility of the rules applicable in the Member States concerning the conflict of laws and of jurisdiction;
- eliminating obstacles to the proper functioning of civil proceedings, if necessary by promoting the compatibility of the rules on civil procedure applicable in the Member States.

Judicial cooperation in criminal matters

The goals set for the development of judicial cooperation in criminal matters are:

- facilitating and accelerating cooperation between competent ministries and judicial or equivalent authorities of the Member States in relation to proceedings and the enforcement of decisions;
- facilitating extradition between Member States;
- ensuring compatibility in rules applicable in the Member States, as may be necessary to improve such cooperation;
- preventing conflicts of jurisdiction between Member States;
- progressively adopting measures establishing minimum rules relating to the constituent elements of criminal acts and penalties in the fields of organised crime, terrorism and illicit drug trafficking.

The objectives remain general and there is no specific timetable. Nevertheless, with a subject as complex as this, the fact that there is now a list of targets to be achieved represents a major first step in judicial cooperation.

Police cooperation

Police cooperation is reflected in joint operations agreed by the Council of the European Union and through Europol.

Common action

Common action includes:

- operational cooperation between the police, customs and other specialised law enforcement services of the Member States in relation to the prevention, detection and investigation of criminal offences;
- the collection, storage, processing, analysis and exchange of relevant information, including information on suspicious financial transactions;
- cooperation and joint initiatives in training, the exchange of liaison officers, secondments, the use of equipment, and forensic research;

- the common evaluation of particular investigative techniques in relation to the detection of serious forms of organised crime.

This list is not exhaustive.

The European Police Office (Europol)

The Council is also required to promote cooperation through Europol and, within five years after the new Treaty has come into force, to adopt measures to enable Europol:

- to facilitate, support and coordinate specific investigative operations by the competent authorities of the Member States;
- to ask the competent authorities of the Member States to conduct their investigations and to develop specific expertise which may be put at the disposal of the Member States to assist them in investigating cases of organised crime;
- to work in close cooperation between prosecuting/investigating officials specialising in the fight against organised crime.

Lastly, the Council is to establish a research, documentation and statistical network on cross-border crime.

Operations carried out in the area of police cooperation (including Europol activities) are subject to appropriate jurisdictional control by the competent authorities under the rules applying in each Member State.

Incorporating the Schengen Area into the European Union

The abolition of border checks within what has been described as the Schengen area became possible because of an initiative by Germany, France and the Benelux countries in 1985. The Schengen Convention of 1990 laid down common rules for visas, the right of asylum, checks at the external borders and cooperation between police forces and customs authorities to allow freedom of movement for individuals within the territories of the signatory countries without disturbing law and order. A reporting system has been set up for the exchange of data about the identity of individuals. Member States of the European Union (apart from the United Kingdom and Ireland), plus Norway and Iceland, have joined this intergovernmental initiative.

Protocol integrating the Schengen acquis into the framework of the European Union

The Member States that are signatories to the Schengen Agreements now conduct 'closer cooperation' on the abolition of internal frontiers within the institutional and legal framework of the European Union. The Council of the European Union has taken the place of the Executive Committee established by the Schengen Agreements. The common rules referred to above have been incorporated either into Title IV of the EC Treaty or into Title VI of the EU Treaty. Until the Council, acting unanimously, has determined the legal basis for each of the provisions or decisions that constitute the Schengen *acquis*, they will be regarded as acts based on Title VI. Any new proposal in the areas of visas, right of asylum, checks at external borders and cooperation between police forces and customs authorities will rely on one of these new bases.

The arrangements will help to further the goal of free movement for persons enshrined in the Single European Act in 1986. At the same time they guarantee democratic control and give citizens channels for appealing to the courts if their rights are called into question (the Court of Justice and/or national courts, depending on the area concerned).

Ireland and the United Kingdom may take part in some or all of the provisions of the Schengen *acquis* after a unanimous vote in the Council by the 13 states that are parties to the Agreements and the representative of the government of the State concerned.

Iceland and Norway are associated with the implementation of the Schengen *acquis* and its further development.

The Schengen acquis

The following acts are described as the Schengen *acquis*:

- the Agreement signed in Schengen on 14 June 1985 between the Benelux countries, Germany and France on the gradual abolition of checks at their common borders;
- the Convention signed in Schengen on 19 June 1990 between Belgium, Germany, France, Luxembourg and the Netherlands implementing the Agreement of 14 June 1985, with related Final Act and common declarations;
- the Accession Protocols and Agreements with Italy (signed on 27 November 1990), Spain and Portugal (signed on 25 June 1991), Greece (signed on 6 November 1992), Austria (signed on 28 April 1959) and Denmark, Finland and Sweden (signed on 19 December 1996), with related Final Acts and declarations;
- decisions and declarations adopted by the Executive Committee established by the 1990 Implementation Convention, as well as acts adopted for the implementation of the Convention by the organs upon which the Executive Committee has conferred decision-making powers.

The renumbering of the Treaties

The entry into force of the Treaty of Amsterdam involves a general renumbering of the titles and articles of the various treaties.

Articles K.1 to K.14 of Title VI of the EU Treaty have been renumbered 29 to 42.

THE UNION AND THE CITIZEN

Citizenship of the European Union

Introduction

As set out in the Maastricht Treaty, any national of a Member State is a citizen of the Union. The aim of European citizenship is to strengthen and consolidate European identity by greater involvement of the citizens in the Community integration process. Thanks to the single market, citizens enjoy a series of general rights in various areas such as the free movement of goods and services, consumer protection and public health, equal opportunities and treatment, access to jobs and social protection. There are four categories of specific provisions and rights attaching to citizenship of the European Union:

- freedom of movement and residence throughout the Union;
- the right to vote and stand as a candidate at municipal elections and in elections to the European Parliament in the State where he resides;
- protection by the diplomatic and consular authorities of any Member State where the State of which the person is a national is not represented in a non-member country;
- the right to petition the European Parliament and apply to the Ombudsman.

Although the exercise of these rights is dependent on European citizenship and is subject to certain limitations laid down by the Treaties or secondary legislation, the right to apply to the Ombudsman or to petition the European Parliament is open to all natural or legal persons residing in the Member States of the Union. Likewise, any person residing in the European Union has fundamental rights.

The Amsterdam Treaty completes the list of civic rights of Union citizens and clarifies the link between national citizenship and European citizenship.

Background

Union citizenship and the rights accompanying it must be seen in perspective in order to understand the dynamics of the process launched by the Treaty setting up the European Economic Community (signed in Rome in 1957). This Treaty gave people the right to move freely within the European Community. Free movement of people was closely linked to economic status as employee, self-employed or service provider. The right of residence throughout the Community was first given to employees and the self-employed and members of their families in conjunction with the right to work there.

The Single European Act (1986) wrote provisions into the Treaty of Rome to establish an area without frontiers and to abolish checks on persons at internal frontiers, irrespective of nationality. Unfortunately, this area was not established before the scheduled date of 31 December 1992. But in 1990 the Council, acting under the Single Act, extended the right of residence to persons who are not engaged in an occupation, provided they have sufficient resources and social insurance cover. The final stage in attaining the general right to movement and residence was its incorporation in the concept of Union citizenship in the Treaty on European Union (1992). In 1997 the Amsterdam Treaty produced a political solution for further progress on free movement, incorporating the Schengen Agreement into the Union Treaty (although some Member States wanted to have special status and will retain controls at their border with other Member States).

As early as the Paris Summit in 1974, attempts had been made to define the 'special rights' to be conferred on nationals of the European Economic Community as it then was. In 1992 the EU Treaty wrote Union citizenship into the Treaty establishing the European Community (Article 17, ex Article 8). After the signing of the Treaty, the declaration by the Birmingham European Council in October 1992 made clear that '... citizenship of the Union brings our citizens additional rights and protection without in any way taking the place of their national citizenship'.

A declaration attached to the Treaty setting up the European Community notes that 'the question whether an individual possesses the nationality of a Member State shall be settled solely by reference to the national law of the Member State concerned'.

The Treaty on European Union, by establishing Union citizenship, confers on every Union citizen a fundamental and personal right to move and reside freely without reference to an economic activity. The right to vote and to stand as a candidate in elections to the European Parliament and in municipal elections in the Member State in which he resides and the right to protection by the diplomatic or consular authorities of any Member State in a non-member country are a concrete expression of the feeling of common citizenship. Directives adopted in 1993 and 1994 laid down the rules for giving effect to these rights. The same Treaty makes it possible to strengthen and amplify these rights.

However, European citizens still encounter real obstacles, both practical and legal, when they wish to exercise their rights to free movement and residence in the Union.

Additions by the Amsterdam Treaty

Amendments have been made to Articles 17 and 21 (ex Articles 8 and 8(d)) of the EC Treaty, which define European citizenship.

Firstly, the Amsterdam clarifies the link between European and national citizenship. It states unequivocally that 'citizenship of the Union shall complement and not replace national citizenship'. Two practical conclusions follow from this:

- it is first necessary to be a national of a Member State in order to enjoy citizenship of the Union;
- European citizenship will supplement and complement the rights conferred by national citizenship.

Moreover, the Amsterdam Treaty has established a new right for European citizens. Every citizen of the Union can now write to the European Parliament, the Council, the Commission, the Court of Justice, the Court of Auditors, the Economic and Social Committee, the Committee of the Regions or the

Ombudsman in one of the 12 languages of the Treaties and receive an answer in the same language.

As a reminder, the 12 languages are: Danish, Dutch, English, Finnish, French, German, Greek, Irish (Gaelic), Italian, Portuguese, Spanish and Swedish.

Lastly, a new paragraph has been inserted in the preamble of the EC Treaty. It confirms the commitment by the Member States to the education of their peoples. Each Member State undertakes 'to promote the development of the highest possible level of knowledge … through a wide access to education and through its continuous updating'.

THE UNION AND THE CITIZEN

Employment

Introduction

Originally the policies and powers of the European Community were not on the agenda of the 1996 Inter-Governmental Conference.

However, the disappointment engendered by the absence of a reference to employment in the Treaty on European Union (1992) and the initiative to combat unemployment mounted by the Essen European Council (9 and 10 December 1994) prompted the Member States to prioritise these issues at the Intergovernmental Conference on the revision of the Treaty of Maastricht, in order to respond to what is one of their citizens' main concerns.

Following difficult negotiations due to the diversity of situations and national policies in the field of employment, a consensus finally emerged on the precedence of national policies and the rejection of large-scale spending programmes. The addition of a new chapter on employment in the Treaty establishing the European Community is the fruit of these negotiations.

A new objective for the European Union

Promoting employment is henceforth one of the objectives of the European Union and becomes a 'matter of common concern' for the Member States (Article 2 of the EC Treaty). The new objective is to achieve 'a high level of employment' without weakening the competitiveness of the European Union (Article 2 of the EU Treaty).

To achieve this objective a new power has been vested in the Union, supplementary to that of the Member States, concerning the preparation of a 'coordinated strategy' for employment. The core of this strategy consists of common guidelines similar to those adopted at the Essen European Council.

The new Title VIII (Articles 125 to 130) of the EC Treaty spells out these objectives and how to achieve them. It also provides for the creation of an Employment Committee.

The Treaty's explicit reference to employment institutionalises the initiatives mounted by the Member States at different European Councils as well as those mounted by the Commission over the past two years.

Moreover, alongside the provisions on economic and monetary union, it redresses the balance by adding to the macroeconomic provisions a number of measures that meet European citizens' expectations as regards the struggle against unemployment.

Indeed one of the hallmarks of this new Title is that repercussions on employment must be taken into account in adopting and implementing each Community policy and action.

Early implementation

At the Amsterdam Council of 16 and 17 June 1997 the Member States decided to apply the new provisions on employment in the Amsterdam Treaty ahead of schedule, and on 1 October the European Commission proposed guidelines for the Member States' employment policies in 1998.

Background

During the Intergovernmental Conference on Economic and Monetary Union (1992), a debate took place on the advisability of including employment among the convergence criteria which Member States had to respect if they wanted to participate in the single currency. This idea was rejected by most governments, who were keen to guard their prerogatives in the field of employment policy. During the national debates in the run-up to the ratification of the Treaty on European Union, the absence of any reference to employment in the new Treaty came in for heavy criticism. It looked as if the European Union cared little about unemployment and jobs — at a time when the Member States were finding themselves compelled to make difficult social choices in order to reduce their deficits in preparation for future economic and monetary union.

Preliminary steps — Essen

In 1994 the Essen European Council (9 and 10 December) adopted — for the first time at European level — short- and medium-term lines of action on employment. The summit's conclusions state that reducing unemployment is one of the priority tasks of the European Union and highlight the structural origins of much of European unemployment and the crucial role of meaningful dialogue between the social partners and policy-makers with a view to resolving this problem.

The European Council also defined five priority strands for Member States' employment policies:

- **promoting investment in vocational training** so that workers can adapt to technological developments throughout their working life;
- **increasing employment** during periods of growth (notably via more flexible work organisation, a wage policy designed to encourage job-creating investments and the encouragement of initiatives at regional and local level);
- **reducing non-wage labour costs** to encourage hiring, in particular of unqualified workers;
- **improving the effectiveness of labour market policy** by a better definition of measures to raise wages and by regularly evaluating the effectiveness of labour market policy instruments;
- improving **measures to help groups which are particularly hard hit** by unemployment, notably long-term unemployment (young people leaving school without qualifications, elderly workers and women).

These recommendations have been implemented in the Member States in the form of multi-annual programmes. Each year the Commission prepares a report on employment trends and policies in the Member States and evaluates them in the light of the priorities that have been adopted.

The Confidence Pact

In June 1996 the European Commission mounted an 'Action for employment in

Europe: a Confidence Pact' with a view to mobilising all the players concerned at Community, national and local level, capitalising on the potential multiplier effect of these actions at European level, and enshrining the struggle against unemployment in the framework of a medium- and long-term vision of society. The Dublin European Council (13 to 14 December 1996) welcomed this initiative, embracing all the economic and social operators and called for swift implementation of the draft territorial employment pacts (80 of these pacts had been signed by June 1997).

The European Union has also taken numerous job-creation measures under the Structural Funds and the European Social Fund. By including employment in the Community policies and putting it on the agenda of all European Councils, the Treaty of Amsterdam allows the development of Community employment initiatives and the creation of a consistent policy at European level.

A new Community Policy

The new Title VIII puts in place a coordinated employment strategy designed to encourage a skilled and adaptable labour force and to promote labour markets that are responsive to economic change.

Common guidelines

Firstly the European Council adopts conclusions on the employment situation in the Community on the basis of the annual report prepared by the Council of the European Union and the Commission.

These conclusions enable the Commission to propose employment policy guidelines each year that are compatible with the major economic guidelines laid down under monetary union (Article 99, ex Article 103). The Council adopts the guidelines by qualified majority after consulting the European Parliament, the Economic and Social Committee, the Committee of the Regions and the Employment Committee. The procedure is modelled on the convergence arrangements for national economic policies. However, the common guidelines do not advocate measures to harmonise national provisions, though they do have an indirect impact on Member States' policy.

Member States must take these common objectives into account in their employment policies. The Council then examines the annual reports submitted by the Member States in this area and, if it deems necessary, addresses a recommendation — acting on a proposal from the Commission — to a Member State. This recommendation is then adopted by the Council by qualified majority.

This provision is similar to the one on economic policy, but no penalties are imposed on Member States that fail to comply with the Council's recommendations. Nor does the Treaty state that these recommendations have to be published.

Finally, in contrast to the provisions on economic and monetary union, Title VIII does not prescribe any macroeconomic objectives to be achieved, along the lines of the economic convergence criteria. Certain Member States did not want binding objectives enshrined in the Treaty. In their view, putting a coordinated strategy in place already amounted to a major step forward.

Incentive measures

The Council may adopt initiative measures to promote employment, acting by qualified majority and in accordance with the co-decision procedure involving the European Parliament. These measures should 'encourage cooperation between Member States and to support their action in the field of employment through initiatives aimed at developing exchanges of information and best practices, providing comparative analysis and advice as well as promoting innovative approaches and evaluating experience, in particular by recourse to pilot projects'. They do not 'include harmonisation of the laws and regulations of the Member States'. However, the coordinated strategy on employment should have an indirect impact on these rules.

The initiative measures are fleshed out in two declarations:

- the actions must specify the grounds for their adoption, their duration (maximum five years) and the maximum amount of funding;
- their funding is limited because it must be provided under Rubric 3 of the Financial Perspectives, which represents approximately 6 % of the Community budget.

The Employment Committee

A Committee on Employment and the Labour Market was established in December 1996. It has restricted powers. The new Article 130 of the EC Treaty replaces this Committee and requires the Council to establish an Employment Committee, on the lines of the Monetary Committee established by economic and monetary union.

This advisory committee promotes coordination between Member States on national employment and labour market policies. It monitors the development of these policies in the Member States and the Community as a whole, formulates opinions either at the request of the Council or Commission or on its own initiative, and helps prepare the ground for the Council's proceedings.

Like the former Committee on Employment and the Labour Market, it consists of two representatives of each Member State and the Commission. It consults the social partners.

THE UNION AND THE CITIZEN

Social policy

Introduction

One of the major innovations introduced by the Treaty of Amsterdam in the European Community's social policy is the incorporation of a strengthened social agreement in the EC Treaty. Already all the directives adopted by the 14 signatories to the agreement have been extended to the United Kingdom.

The 'reunification of the 15' restores unity and cohesion to the Community's social policy. It should encourage more frequent reliance on the social provisions of the EC Treaty and should broaden the policy's remit. Essentially, the Social Agreement has been incorporated as it stands. However, some provisions have been strengthened, especially those on equal opportunities and combating social exclusion.

The foundations of social policy

The new Treaty provides for the merger of the two legal bases on which social policy previously rested:

- the EC Treaty, which contains provisions applicable to all Member States (Title IX, ex Title VIII);
- the Social Agreement annexed to the Social Protocol, which contains provisions concerning the 14 signatory Member States.

Article 136 (ex Article 117) reaffirms that social policy is a competence which the European Community shares with the Member States. However, even if the Community's main role is to support and complement the activities of the Member States, incorporation of the Social Agreement substantially extends its powers in this area.

Moreover, the Community and the Member States have defined the social rights they hold to be fundamental on the basis of two texts:

- the European Social Charter signed at Turin on 18 October 1961;
- the 1989 Community Charter of the Fundamental Social Rights of Workers.

These fundamental social rights mainly concern employment, living and working conditions, social protection, social dialogue and the combating of exclusion.

Integration of the Social Agreement

A Social Agreement was concluded at the intergovernmental conference on political union in 1992. The United Kingdom decided to opt out. However, the 12 Member States at the time adopted a protocol, annexed to the Treaty of Maastricht, authorising the other 11 Member States to apply, without the United Kingdom, a more ambitious text than the chapter on Community social policy. This text was based on the Social Charter adopted in 1989 by all the Member States save the United Kingdom.

The Social Protocol has been repealed and the Social Agreement incorporated into the provisions of Title IX of the EC Treaty. The European Community can now act or reinforce its action in the following areas:

- improvement of the working environment to protect workers' health and safety;
- working conditions;
- information and consultation of workers;
- integration of persons excluded from the labour market;
- equality between men and women.

To this list, already present in the Social Agreement, the Treaty of Amsterdam adds the possibility of adopting initiatives specifically designed to combat social exclusion.

However, as in the past, remuneration, the right of association, and the right to strike or lock out are not addressed at Community level.

The extension of codecision to certain areas

While the Community's remit is not broadened to any great extent, the legislative process has changed in the areas indicated above.

Taking account of the conditions and technical rules that apply in each of the Member States, the Council may adopt directives by qualified majority under the co-decision procedure, after consulting the Economic and Social Committee and the Committee of the Regions.

Using the same procedure, the Council may also adopt measures to encourage cooperation between Member States in developing exchanges of information, promoting innovative approaches and evaluating experiences in order to combat social exclusion.

The maintenance of unanimity in the other areas

The following areas defined by the Social Protocol are being introduced under Title IX. The decision-making procedure remains unchanged.

Here the Council acts unanimously on a proposal from the Commission, after consulting the European Parliament and the Economic and Social Committee. The only difference between this and the Social Agreement procedure is that the Committee of the Regions is also consulted.

This procedure applies to the following points:

- social security and social protection of workers;
- protection of workers when their employment contract is terminated;
- representation and collective defence of the interests of workers and employers (including co-determination);
- employment conditions for third-country nationals legally resident in Community territory;
- financial contributions for promotion of employment and job-creation (without prejudice to the provisions relating to the Social Fund).

Finally, it should be noted that measures adopted at Community level do not prevent Member States from introducing more stringent protective measures, provided they are compatible with Community law.

The social partners

The fundamental role of the social partners has been enshrined in the Social Agreement and the provisions contained in this agreement have been fully embodied in the Treaty of Amsterdam.

The Commission facilitates dialogue between the social partners and consults them on the content of proposals in the social field before presenting them.

The social partners are involved throughout the legislative process, and this allows them to play a substantial role both in drafting and implementing new measures. Indeed each Member State can leave it to the social partners to implement the new directives.

Equal opportunities and equal treatment

Up to now the Treaty required Member States to ensure equal pay for men and women for equal work. With the Treaty of Amsterdam, a new legal basis has been introduced for measures on equal opportunities and equal treatment of men and women at work.

After consulting the Economic and Social Committee, the Council can adopt positive measures to ensure that the principle is applied, acting under the co-decision procedure. The Member States, too, are free to make specific concessions to allow men or women easier access to occupations where one sex is under-represented. But the measures taken must not involve rigid quotas, because the Court of Justice outlawed these in its Kalanka judgment of 1995 (the Court also addressed the issue in a judgment in 1997, in the Marshall case).

THE UNION AND THE CITIZEN

Environment

Introduction

Environment policy is one of the greatest social challenges facing the public authorities and all sectors of the economy today. It is also a subject of which the public is acutely aware, since it directly affects its welfare and health.

From the 1970s onwards the concern to conserve the environment started to give birth to a series of Community initiatives. However, the European Union internal market was criticised for putting the economic aspects and trade before protection of the environment, which was perceived as a potential barrier to trade rather than as an end in itself. In response to these criticisms the Treaty on European Union upgraded the environment to a Community policy and no longer simply action by the Community.

However, the EU Treaty was itself open to certain criticism, notably for its failure to simplify the decision-making procedures that applied to environment policy. Sometimes, too, a conflict of legal basis arose between the 'environment procedure' (Article 175, ex Article 130s, of the EC Treaty) and the 'approximation of laws' procedure for the internal market (Article 95, ex Article 100a, of the EC Treaty). This could often make a difference in terms of how strictly the Member States interpreted and implemented the rules. Another charge levelled at the EU Treaty was that it did not explicitly incorporate the commitment to sustainable development made at the 1992 Rio Conference but merely included a passing reference to sustainable growth and respect for the environment.

The Treaty of Amsterdam answers these problems. Sustainable development is enshrined as one of the Union's tasks, together with the principle of integrating the environment into other policies. The decision-making procedures are now clearer and more efficient.

Background

In the early days of building Europe, environmental issues were not a top priority for the public authorities and economic circles.

It was not until the 1970s that the emergence of environmental concerns triggered moves in this area at Community level. At the July 1972 Paris Summit the Heads of State and Government recognised that in the context of economic expansion and improving the quality of life, particular attention should be paid to the environment.

Consequently, the signal was given and the first action programme setting out the framework for Community environment policy was adopted, covering the period from 1973 to 1976. This was followed by other multiannual programmes of the same type which led to the adoption of a series of directives on protection of natural resources (air and water), noise abatement, nature conservation and waste management.

However, the entry into force of the Single European Act in 1987, adding a title specifically on the subject to the Treaty establishing the European Community, is generally acknowledged as the turning-point for the environment. From then on, the Community measures had a legal basis explicitly defining the objectives and guiding principles for action by the European Community relating to the environment. And provision was made for environmental protection requirements to become a component of the Community's other policies.

The entry into force of the EU Treaty in November 1993 brought further progress on several fronts. First it added the concept of 'sustainable growth respecting the environment' to the European Community's tasks and wrote the precautionary principle into the article on which environment policy is founded (Article 174, ex Article 130r, of the EC Treaty). Beyond that, it upgraded action on the environment to the status of a 'policy' in its own right and made qualified majority voting in the Council the general rule. The only exceptions are matters such as environmental taxes, town and country planning and land use, where unanimity remains the norm. As for the co-decision procedure, this was confined to issues concerning the internal market.

In the final analysis, in the course of building Europe provisions commensurate with the high stakes represented by the environment have gradually been evolved. Nevertheless, this progress, step by step, also created certain inconsistencies, such as the conflicting legal bases or the different decision-making procedures. The Treaty of Amsterdam should resolve these problems and respond to the need to make Community environment policy clearer and more efficient.

Sustainable development and taking the environment into account in all policies

The EU Treaty lays down that 'environmental protection requirements must be integrated into the definition and implementation of other Community policies'. This is a *sine qua non* for sustainable growth respecting the environment.

The Treaty of Amsterdam seeks to provide stronger guarantees than given by the Single Act and the Treaty on European Union, by inserting the concept of sustainable development plus a new article in the Treaty establishing the European Community.

Introduction of the principle of sustainable development

This principle is now enshrined in the preamble and in the objectives of the EU Treaty. It also features in Article 2 of the EC Treaty, which lays down the tasks of the Community.

New Article 6 of the EC Treaty

The new Article 6 puts at the start of the Treaty the clause calling for environmental protection requirements to be integrated into the definition and implementation of other policies. This was already contained in Article 174 (ex Article 130r). The new article also cites such integration as one means of promoting sustainable development.

This new article must be seen in conjunction with the declaration on environmental impact assessments, annexed to the Final

Act of the Intergovernmental Conference which drafted the Treaty of Amsterdam. In this declaration the Conference notes that the Commission undertakes to prepare environmental impact assessment studies when making proposals which may have significant environmental implications.

The environment and approximation of laws on the internal market

To smooth the way for completion of the internal market, the Single European Act allowed the Council to take decisions approximating laws between the Member States by a qualified majority. A parallel framework was created for free movement, reflecting the need to take account of issues of vital importance for society such as the environment, public health or consumer protection (Article 95(3), ex Article 100a(3), of the EC Treaty). The Treaty of Amsterdam further strengthens this framework.

Amendment of the provisions on approximation of laws

The EC Treaty now requires all proposals by the Commission to be based on a high level of environmental protection. Previously, after a harmonisation measure had been adopted by the Council, any Member State could still apply different national provisions if warranted by major environmental protection requirements. The Member State in question had to notify the Commission, which then verified that the provisions involved were not a means of arbitrary discrimination or a disguised restriction on trade between the Member States.

This mechanism has now been extended, drawing a distinction between two separate cases (Article 95, ex Article 100a). After a Community harmonisation measure has been adopted, Member States may:

- either maintain existing national provisions to protect the environment; or
- introduce new national provisions to protect the environment.

In the first case, the Member State must notify the Commission and give its reasons for maintaining those national provisions.

In the second case, the Member State must again notify the Commission of the new national provisions and explain its reasons for introducing them. Moreover, those measures must be based on new scientific evidence and must be in response to a problem that specifically affects the Member State in question and that arose after the harmonisation measure was adopted.

In both cases, the Commission checks whether or not the national measures involved are a means of arbitrary discrimination, a disguised restriction on trade between Member States, or an obstacle to the functioning of the internal market.

The Commission has six months to decide whether to approve or reject the measure. This may be extended by a further six months in certain circumstances. In the absence of a decision, the national provisions are deemed to have been approved.

The environment and decision-making at Community level

Decision-making in the Treaty on European Union

The EU Treaty established a more efficient decision-making procedure for environment policy, replacing unanimity in the Council by qualified majority voting as the general rule. However, the arrangements were still complex, with several different procedures existing side by side:

- the co-decision procedure for general action programmes;
- the cooperation procedure for the environment policy;
- simple consultation, with unanimous adoption by the Council, for measures concerning taxation, town and country planning, land use, or energy supply.

In addition, there was sometimes a grey area between environmental measures (Article 175, ex Article 130s) and the approximation of laws in connection with the internal market (Article 95, ex Article 100a). Since the co-decision procedure applies to the approximation of laws, there was a risk of conflict between Article 100a and Article 130s as the legal basis for action relating to the environment.

Simplification of decision-making and the Treaty of Amsterdam

The entry into force of the Treaty of Amsterdam has simplified the situation, replacing the cooperation procedure by the co-decision procedure. This reorganisation has the advantage of reducing the number of procedures to two (the Member States still wished to retain unanimity for the fields indicated above). This makes the Treaty more readable and reduces the risk of conflicts over the legal basis.

THE UNION AND THE CITIZEN

Public health

Introduction

The Single European Act and the emergence of the concept of a Citizens' Europe added new concerns such as the environment, health and consumer protection to the Treaty of Rome, alongside the priority of securing free movement.

As far as health protection is concerned, the EU Treaty provided a major impetus by introducing a specific article on public health into the EC Treaty — Article 129 (now renumbered Article 152).

However, since most power in this sector remains in the hands of the Member States, the Community's role is subsidiary and mainly involves supporting the efforts of the Member States and helping them formulate and implement coordinated objectives and strategies.

Problems as manifold as drug addiction or blood transfusion chains in the Member States have however highlighted the fact that national policies may sometimes have repercussions far beyond national frontiers. Certain public health problems call for an international response and hence close cooperation between the Member States.

The Treaty of Amsterdam is designed to improve matters by amending the wording of Article 152 (ex Article 129) of the EC Treaty.

Background

Originally the Treaty of Rome did not contain any formal legal basis for measures in the field of public health. However, since 1997, a Council of the Ministers of Health began to meet on an occasional basis. These meetings resulted in acts such as 'decisions of the Member States meeting within the Council' or non-binding resolutions. Following the signature of the Single European Act, instruments of this kind — whose legal impact is sometimes uncertain — began to proliferate. Public health was finally enshrined in the Treaty on European Union with the insertion of a 'Public health' Title, which opened the way to formal cooperation between Member States in this area. In parallel, Article 3 raised health protection to the rank of a Community objective.

Since then Community measures have focused on horizontal initiatives providing for information, education, surveillance and training in the field of health, the drafting by the European Commission of reports on the state of health in the European Community and the integration of health protection requirements into Community policies. Moreover, global multiannual programmes have been mounted in priority areas such as cancer, drug addiction, AIDS and transmissible diseases.

Community action has also assumed other forms, for example in the fields of transmissible diseases, blood and tobacco and — in the context of completing the Single Market — through the adoption of legislation on veterinary and phytosanitary controls, or again, in the field of biotechnology, through the funding of research work.

The new Article 152 of the EC Treaty

The Community can now adopt measures aimed at ensuring (rather than merely contributing to) a high level of human health protection.

The new Article 152 (ex Article 129) of the EC Treaty has a wider scope than before. Among the areas of cooperation between Member States, the new Article lists not only diseases and major health scourges but also, more generally, all causes of danger to human health, as well as the general objective of improving health.

The Council may also adopt measures setting high quality and safety standards for organs and substances of human origin, blood and blood derivatives. Veterinary and plant-health measures directly aimed at protecting public health are now adopted under the co-decision procedure. This is a new departure, as the European Parliament previously only had a right to be consulted on the adoption of health measures linked to agriculture.

THE UNION AND THE CITIZEN

Consumer protection

Introduction

With the adoption of the Single European Act and the emergence of the concept of Citizens' Europe, concerns such as the environment, health and consumer protection were enshrined in the Treaty of Rome, alongside the priority of freedom of movement.

The EU Treaty marked a new departure with the introduction of a specific article on consumers into the EC Treaty (Article 129a, now renumbered Article 153).

More recently, the 'mad cow' crisis has led to calls for stronger action by the European Union to protect consumers and for better consumer information.

The Treaty of Amsterdam attempts to meet these expectations and to respond more effectively, and so the wording of Article 153 (ex Article 129a) of the EC Treaty has been altered.

The provisions on consumers have been improved, clarifying the Community's objectives and linking them more closely with the other policies.

The background

Initially the Treaty of Rome contained no formal legal basis for consumer protection. But long before the formal adoption of former Article 129a, the Community began to concern itself with this issue.

An example is the 1979 Directive on consumer protection as regards food price labelling, which was based on Article 235 (now Article 308) of the EC Treaty, and the Directives on misleading advertising (1984) and the protection of consumers in the case of contracts negotiated away from business premises (1985), based on Article 100 (now Article 94) of that Treaty.

Since the advent of Single European Act and the introduction of Article 100a (now Article 95) into the EC Treaty, the Commission's proposals on the approximation of laws affecting the internal market must be based on a high level of consumer protection.

A certain number of texts have been based on this Article, notably the directives on package travel, package holidays and package tours (1990) and unfair terms in consumer contracts (1993).

A further impetus was given by the Intergovernmental Conference preceding the adoption of the Treaty on European Union, with the introduction of a specific title on consumer protection into the EC Treaty.

Since then the Community has redoubled its efforts to ensure a high level of consumer protection.

The Community has endeavoured to protect the health and economic interests of consumers through a range of specific measures.

Examples include the directive on price labelling of products offered to consumers (the first directive based on Article 129a, now Article 153), the 1997 directive amending the 1984 directive on misleading advertising so as to include comparative advertising, and the 1997 directive on the protection of consumers in respect of contracts negotiated at a distance, both based on Article 100a (now Article 95).

The new Article 153 of the EC Treaty

The Community now has greater scope for adopting preventive measures in the field of consumer protection.

The new Article 153 (ex Article 129a) of the EC Treaty has the objective of ensuring a high level of consumer protection, rather than simply contributing to such protection. Moreover, it emphasises promoting the consumers' right to information and education and their right to organise themselves in order to safeguard their interests.

THE UNION AND THE CITIZEN

Transparency, simplification of the Treaties and quality of Community legislation

Introduction

The European Union often deals with complex technical matters, whilst its institutional arrangements are unique and difficult to understand on first acquaintance. Frequent misunderstandings have thus arisen between the European institutions, national political and economic interests and the European public at large. To promote a better understanding of the European integration process, the institutions are gradually adopting more transparent ways of working and taking decisions.

The concept of 'transparency' applies mainly to the question of access to Union information and documents, but it also has to do with the production of clearly understandable legislative texts. It involves not only producing a single consolidated version of each text which has undergone amendments (such consolidation may be done formally or informally) but also laying down drafting rules so that any piece of legislation adopted in each of the Community's official languages (of which there are currently 11) is as clear as possible.

The Treaty of Amsterdam confers certain rights on the public and makes recommendations to the institutions with a view to ensuring that the fullest possible information is available and thus improving the democratic workings of the European Union.

Transparency

To clarify the concept of 'transparency' some amendments have been made to the EC Treaty.

A new Article 255 has been inserted, giving any Union citizen and any natural or legal person residing or having a registered office in a Member State the right of access to European Parliament, Council and Commission documents.

The general principles governing the right of access and any restrictions on the grounds of public or private interest are to be fixed by the Council, acting under the co-decision procedure with Parliament, within two years after the Treaty of Amsterdam enters into force. The three institutions concerned must include specific rules on access to documents in their rules of procedure.

A third paragraph has been added to Article 207 (ex Article 151), requiring the Council to grant access to documents relating to its legislative activities. As a minimum requirement, the results of votes, explanations of votes, and statements in the minutes must be made public.

These provisions clarify the rights of the public regarding access to documents and apply to all areas covered by the first and third pillars. However, they do not cover the common foreign and security policy, since that involves diplomatic rather than legislative activities. Access to certain national documents may also be restricted if the Member State concerned so requests (declaration adopted by the Intergovernmental Conference on Article 255).

Simplification and consolidation of the Treaties

It has become difficult to read the original Treaties because of all the deletions, additions and amendments made by the Single European Act and the Treaties of Maastricht and Amsterdam. To make the EU Treaty and the EC Treaty easier to follow, all their articles have been renumbered.

In a declaration adopted by the Intergovernmental Conference, the Member States also agreed to produce consolidated versions of all the Treaties. This consolidation will have no legal status but will provide more legible texts from which any lapsed provisions will have been deleted.

Quality of the drafting of Community legislation

The Intergovernmental Conference adopted a declaration incorporating the conclusions of the Edinburgh European Council (11 to 12 December 1992) and the Council Resolution of 8 June 1993.

This declaration stresses that Community legislation must be clearly drafted if it is to be properly implemented by the competent national authorities and better understood by the general public.

In particular, the Conference calls on the three main institutions responsible for drafting Community legislation (the European Parliament, the Council and the Commission) to establish guidelines for improving the quality of the texts which they draft, amend or adopt.

The Conference also called for the codification of legislative texts to be speeded up.

AN EFFECTIVE AND COHERENT EXTERNAL POLICY

Common foreign and security policy

Introduction

One of the main purposes of the Intergovernmental Conference which led to the signature of the draft Amsterdam Treaty was to make common foreign and security policy (CFSP) more effective and to equip the Union better for its role in international politics.

The reform seemed particularly urgent after the disintegration of former Yugoslavia. The tragic course of events there made it clear that the Union needed to be able to act to avert disaster and not merely react after the event. The Yugoslav crisis also threw into relief the weakness of uncoordinated Member State reactions.

The Amsterdam Treaty aims to overcome contradictions between the particularly ambitious objectives of the CFSP and the means available to the Union for achieving those objectives, which did not live up to expectations or provide adequately for the matters at stake.

Background

Throughout the successive stages of the construction of a European Community, the issues of political union, common foreign policy and common defence policy have regularly been put on the agenda by a series of policy proposals.

In 1950, the Pléven plan (named after the French Prime Minister) was to create an integrated European army under joint command. This plan was the subject of negotiation between Member States of the European Coal and Steel Community from 1950 to 1952, and led to the signature of the Treaty establishing the European Defence Community (EDC).

The corollary of the EDC was a political project, presented in 1953, for creating a federal or confederative structure. The 'European Political Community' would have created a two-house Parliamentary assembly, a European Executive Council, a Council of Ministers and a Court of Justice. The Political Community was to have very wide powers and responsibilities and was, in the long run, to absorb the ECSC and the EDC. However, it never came to fruition, since it was rejected by the French National Assembly on 30 August 1954.

In the early 1960s, tough negotiations were conducted on the basis of the two Fouchet plans presented one after the other in France, calling for closer political cooperation, a Union of States and common foreign and defence policies. A committee established to draft specific proposals produced difficult, but nevertheless ambitious, compromises such as setting up an independent secretariat and the introduction of qualified majority decisions on certain issues as a long-term goal. Unfortunately agreement could not be reached on the proposals of the Fouchet Committee and negotiations between the Member States foundered in 1962.

In response to calls by Heads of State or Government for a study of possible ways of moving forward on the political level, the 'Davignon report' was presented in 1970 at the Luxembourg Summit. This was the starting point for European Political Cooperation (EPC) launched informally in 1970 before being formally enshrined in the Single European Act (SEA) in 1987. The main feature of EPC was consultation among the Member States on foreign policy issues.

Three years later, the Copenhagen Summit presented a report on how EPC was working. Subsequently, meetings of foreign ministers and the Political Committee (made up of national political directors) were held more frequently. At the same time, a group of 'European correspondents' was set up to monitor EPC in each Member State. Political cooperation was also assisted by access to COREU, the new telex network linking the Member States.

The establishment of the European Council in 1974 contributed to better coordination of EPC because of the role it gave to Heads of State or Government in defining the general orientation of Community policy. From that point on the role of the Presidency and the publicity given to the work of the EPC reinforced each other through official Community statements of position.

The Soviet invasion of Afghanistan and the Islamic revolution in Iran brought home to the Member States the growing impotence of the European Community on the international scene. Determined to strengthen EPC, in 1981 they adopted the London Report which required prior consultation by Member States with each other and the European Commission on all foreign policy matters affecting all Member States. In 1982, prompted by the same concern to affirm the international position of the Community, the Genscher–Colombo initiative proposed a draft 'European Act' and led, in 1983, to the Stuttgart 'Solemn Declaration on European Union'.

In 1985 the Dooge Committee Report, drawn up in preparation for the Intergovernmental Conference which was to lead to the Single European Act, contained a number of proposals concerning foreign policy, in particular for greater concertation of policy on matters concerning security, and for cooperation in the armaments sector. It also called for the creation of a permanent Secretariat. In the end, the provisions introduced by the Single European Act did not go as far as the Dooge Committee proposals, but they did establish an institutional basis for EPC, the group of European correspondents and a Secretariat working under the direct authority of the Presidency. The objectives of EPC were also extended to all foreign policy issues of general interest.

The Intergovernmental Conference on political union led to the inclusion in the EU Treaty of a specific Title on a common foreign and security policy (CFSP). With the Treaty's entry into force in 1993, the CFSP replaced EPC and a separate intergovernmental pillar was created in the Community structure. This expressed the will of the Union to assert its identity on the international scene.

Title V of the Treaty on European Union

Common foreign and security policy (CFSP) is governed by the provisions of Title V of the Treaty on European Union. The CFSP is also addressed in Article 2 (ex Article B) of the Common Provisions, which states that one of the objectives of the

Union is to 'assert its identity on the international scene, in particular through the implementation of a common foreign and security policy, including the eventual framing of a common defence policy, which might in time lead to a common defence'.

The CFSP was introduced as the result of a desire to equip the Union better for the many challenges facing it at international level, by providing it with new means of taking action in areas of foreign relations other than the traditional Community ones (mainly trade policy and development cooperation).

Title V constitutes a separate pillar of the European Union, since the way it operates and its intergovernmental nature distinguish it from the traditional pillars of the Community, such as the single market and trade policy. This difference is most striking in the decision-making procedures, which require Member State consensus, whereas in traditional Community areas a majority vote suffices. Other differences are the less important roles played by the Commission, the European Parliament and the Court of Justice in matters falling under Title V. The backgrounding of these institutions under the CFSP is in stark contrast with their powers and responsibilities in traditional spheres of Community competence.

To achieve harmony and avoid contradictions between these two types of activity (Community and intergovernmental), Article 3 (ex Article C) provides that: 'The Union shall ensure (...) the consistency of its external activities as a whole in the context of its external relations, security, economic and development policies. The Council and the Commission shall be responsible for ensuring such consistency. They shall assure the implementation of these policies, each in accordance with its respective powers'.

Nevertheless, in the first years after its introduction, Member States' joint action under Title V did not work as satisfactorily as they might have hoped. It was against this relatively unsatisfactory background that the negotiations at the 1996 Intergovernmental Conference aimed to introduce in the new Treaty the institutional reforms needed to make the CFSP effective.

Progress under the Treaty of Amsterdam

First and foremost, the CFSP's capacity for action has been reinforced through the introduction of more coherent instruments and more efficient decision-making. It is now possible to adopt measures by a qualified majority vote, with the dual safeguards of 'constructive abstention' and the possibility of referring a decision to the European Council if a Member State resorts to a veto. The Commission, for its part, is also more involved both on the representative side and in implementation.

Common strategies

The Amsterdam Treaty has added a new foreign policy instrument to the existing ones (joint action and common position), namely common strategies.

The European Council, the body that defines the principles and general guidelines of the CFSP, now has the right to define, by consensus, common strategies in areas where the Member States have important interests in common. The objectives, duration, and means to be made available by the Union and Member States for such common strategies must be specified.

The Council is responsible for implementing common strategies through joint actions and common positions adopted by a qualified majority. It also recommends common strategies to the European Council.

Decision-making

The general rule remains that CFSP decisions always require a unanimous vote in their favour. However, Member States can exercise 'constructive abstention', that is, an abstention which does not block the adoption of the decision. If they qualify their abstention by a formal declaration, they are not obliged to apply the decision; but they must accept, in a spirit of solidarity, that the decision commits the Union as a whole and must agree to abstain from any action that might conflict with the Union's action under that decision.

This mechanism does not apply if the Member States abstaining in this way account for more than one third of Council votes weighted in accordance with the Treaty.

The amended Title V of the EU Treaty does, however, allow for adoption by a qualified majority in two cases:

- for decisions applying a common strategy defined by the European Council;
- for any decisions implementing a joint action or common position already adopted by the Council.

There is a safeguard clause enabling Member States to block majority voting for important reasons of national policy. In such cases, when the Member State concerned has stated its reasons, the Council may decide by a qualified majority to refer the matter to the European Council for a unanimous decision by Heads of State or Government.

The High Representative for the CFSP

The new Article 26 (ex Article J.16) of the EU Treaty introduces a new post intended to give the CFSP a higher profile and make it more coherent.

The Secretary-General of the Council has been assigned the role of High Representative for the CFSP. He is responsible for assisting the Council in CFSP-related matters by contributing to the formulation, preparation, and implementation of decisions. At the request of the Presidency he acts on behalf of the Council in conducting political dialogue with third parties.

Because of this new role, the Secretary-General's administrative tasks have been transferred to the deputy Secretary-General. It does not, however, stop the Council appointing special representatives with mandates covering specific political issues whenever it sees fit, as has already been done in the case of former Yugoslavia.

As regards the logistics of the new position, the High Representative is supported by a policy planning and early warning unit set up in the General Secretariat of the Council and placed under his responsibility.

The policy planning and early warning unit

The coherence of common foreign and security policy depends how Member States react to international developments. Past experience has shown that if reactions are uncoordinated, the position of the European Union and its Member States on the international scene is weakened. Joint analysis of international issues and their impact, and pooling of information should help the Union produce effective reactions to international developments.

With this in mind, it was agreed in a declaration annexed to the Treaty of Amsterdam to set up a policy planning and early warning unit in the General Secretariat of the Council under the authority of the High Representative for the CFSP. Comprising specialists drawn from the General Secretariat, the Member States, the Commission and the Western European Union (WEU), its tasks include:

- monitoring and analysing developments in areas relevant to the CFSP;
- providing assessments of the Union's foreign and security policy interests and identifying areas on which the CFSP could focus in future;
- providing timely assessments and early warning of events, potential political crises and situations that might have significant repercussions on the CFSP;
- producing, at the request of either the Council or the Presidency, or on its own initiative, reasoned policy option papers for the Council.

The 'Petersberg tasks', security and the Western European Union

The 'Petersberg tasks' have been incorporated into Title V of the EU Treaty. This is a crucial step forward at a time when there has been a resurgence of local conflicts posing a real threat to European security (for example, former Yugoslavia), even though the risk of large-scale conflicts has fallen significantly compared to the cold war period.

The 'Petersberg tasks' represent a very fitting response by the Union, embodying as they do the Member States' shared determination to safeguard European security through operations such as humanitarian and peace-making missions.

On the security front, the new Article 17 (ex Article J.7) of the EU Treaty also opens up prospects for two new developments, although neither seems imminent:

- common defence; and
- the integration of the Western European Union (WEU) into the European Union.

Specifically, the new text states that the CFSP covers all questions relating to the security of the Union, including the progressive framing of a common defence policy, which might lead to common defence, should the European Council so decide. Similarly, as regards rapprochement of the EU and the WEU, provision is made for the Union fostering closer institutional relations with the WEU with a view to the possible integration of the WEU into the European Union, should the European Council so decide.

Financing of CFSP operational expenditure

Under the EU Treaty, CFSP operations were financed either from the Community budget or by the Member States, applying a scale to be decided case by case. This system gave rise to some criticism, particularly from the Commission, because of its complexity and inefficiency.

The Treaty of Amsterdam has addressed the problem, providing for expenditure on CFSP operations to be financed from the Community budget. The only exceptions are operations with military or defence implications, or if the Council unanimously decides otherwise. In this case, Member States that abstain and issue a formal declaration are not obliged to contribute to the financing of the operation.

Where expenditure is charged to the Member States, the cost is divided according to gross national product, unless the Council unanimously decides otherwise.

AN EFFECTIVE AND COHERENT EXTERNAL POLICY

Common commercial policy

Introduction

As part of the European Community, the Member States have established a customs union with common arrangements for imports from other countries. The Community's common commercial policy is therefore based on a common external tariff uniformly applied to all Member States.

When the EEC Treaty was signed, the Community's economy and external trade were geared mainly to production and trade in industrial products. This no longer applies, because the services sector is now the main source of jobs within the European Union and accounts for a substantial proportion of its international trade. This change is due partly to very stiff competition from newly industrialised countries in traditional sectors and partly to the economic changes brought about by the new information and communication technologies.

Following the Uruguay Round negotiations under the GATT, the setting-up of the World Trade Organisation (WTO) clearly reflected this trend. In order to cope with the changing nature of trade, the WTO embraces, within the same structure, trade negotiations on products (GATT), services (GATS) and intellectual property (TRIPS).

In the face of the new pattern of international trade, the European Union must be able to develop its trade mechanisms rapidly if it wishes to maintain its leading role in world trade relations. The scope of Article 113 (renumbered Article 133) is still rather vague and until it takes account of the globalisation of trade negotiations, the EU will continue to create difficulties for itself *vis-à-vis* its trading partners.

The Amsterdam Treaty is intended to clarify the situation by providing the Union with the means of extending the common commercial policy, where applicable, to services and intellectual property rights.

Background

The objective of the EEC Treaty was to establish a common market between the Member States of the Community in which goods, people, services and capital could move freely. In order to achieve this, a 12-year transitional period up to 31 December 1969 was introduced. For the sake of cohesion, liberalisation at internal level had to be in tune with that at external level and the Community therefore has had sole competence for common commercial policy since the transitional period ended.

Up to 1970, it was for Member States to coordinate their trade relations with non-Community countries. This did not, however, prevent the Community from concluding bilateral agreements (e.g. with Israel in 1964) or from taking part, in its own right, in the Kennedy Round of negotiations between 1963 and 1967.

Gradually, the expansion of international trade made common commercial policy into one of the Community's most important policies. At the same time, the successive enlargements of the Community and the consolidation of the common market strengthened the Community's position as a pole of attraction and influence for trade negotiations, conducted bilaterally with other countries and multilaterally in the GATT. The EU therefore gradually developed a close network of trade relations world wide, and as a result the EU is now at the top of the international trade league, ahead of the United States and Japan.

Since 1 January 1970, decisions under common commercial policy have been taken by qualified majority within the Council. The scope of Article 113 has been given a wide interpretation by the Court of Justice, which in 1978 stated that the list in Article 113(1) was not restrictive (it refers to changes in tariff rates, the conclusion of tariff and trade agreements, the achievement of uniformity in measures of liberalisation, export policy and measures to protect trade). The Court also felt that commercial policy would gradually lose its importance if it was not allowed to go beyond the traditional machinery of external trade. The Court added to its interpretation in 1994, however, by stating that trade negotiations on services and intellectual property could not be based on Article 113 and so did not come under the Community's sole powers. The Court nevertheless stressed the need for close cooperation between the Commission and Member States and recommended that a code of conduct be adopted.

The new Article 133 of the EC Treaty

A new paragraph has been added to Article 133 (ex Article 113). It allows the Council, after consulting Parliament, to extend the scope of Article 133 to international negotiations and agreements on services and intellectual property rights where they are not already covered by common commercial policy.

The addition of this paragraph means that it will not be necessary to amend the Treaty (which would require an intergovernmental conference and ratification by all the Member States) if it is decided to extend the scope of the traditional trade negotiation procedure.

In concrete terms, a decision to extend the Community's powers in trade matters can now be taken by the members of the Council acting unanimously.

INSTITUTIONAL MATTERS

The European Parliament

Introduction

Enlargement of the European Union into central and eastern Europe will entail changes in the workings of the European institutions. The present structure is that of an organisation set up for six Member States and although it has undergone adjustments to take account of the accession of new Member States, it is still working on the basis of the same institutional principles.

The Intergovernmental Conference which drew up the Treaty of Amsterdam was endeavouring both to confer greater democratic legitimacy on the European institutions and to improve the efficiency of the institutional framework in anticipation of enlargement. The wider role accorded to the European Parliament following the entry into force of the Treaty of Amsterdam will allow the first of these objectives to be met. However, a further intergovernmental conference will be necessary to prepare the institutions for the accession of new Member States. This is provided for in a protocol annexed to the Treaties.

The European Parliament now has a greater say in the European Union's decision-making process. The legislative procedures have been simplified and reduced in number. The new Treaty provides for the virtual abolition of the cooperation procedure and a substantial extension of the co-decision procedure, thus giving the European Parliament equal legislative powers with the Council.

Co-decision procedure

Extension of co-decision

The scope of the co-decision procedure, involving both Parliament and the Council, has been widened substantially. It is now the general rule both for matters where qualified majority voting applies and for the new areas brought into the Treaty for the first time. The one exception is agriculture, where the Council decides by a qualified majority but needs only to consult Parliament. Co-decision also applies to certain questions where the Council decides by unanimous vote. The cooperation procedure is required only for certain decisions relating to economic and monetary union.

To be precise, the co-decision procedure has been extended to cover the following areas of the EC Treaty (the article numbers reflect the new numbering):

- prohibition of any discrimination on grounds of nationality (Article 12);
- right to move and reside freely within the territory of the European Union (Article 18(2));
- social security for migrant workers (Article 42);

- right of establishment for foreign nationals (Article 46(2));
- arrangements for the professions (Article 47(2));
- implementation of the common transport policy (Articles 71 and 80);
- incentives for employment (Article 129);
- certain provisions from the 'Social Agreement' incorporated into the EC Treaty by the Treaty of Amsterdam;
- customs cooperation (Article 135);
- measures to combat social exclusion (Article 137(2));
- equal opportunities and equal treatment (Article 141);
- implementing decisions relating to the European Social Fund (Article 148);
- vocational training (Article 150(4));
- public health (Article 152);
- certain provisions relating to trans-European networks (Article 156);
- implementing decisions relating to the European Regional Development Fund (Article 162);
- research (Article 172);
- environment (Article 175(1));
- development cooperation (Article 179);
- transparency (Article 255);
- measures to combat fraud (Article 280);
- statistics (Article 285);
- establishment of an advisory body on data protection (Article 286).

Simplification of the co-decision procedure

The procedure introduced by the Maastricht Treaty involved up to three readings of legislative proposals in the Council if disagreement persisted between it and the European Parliament. If the Council and Parliament had not reached agreement after the second reading, the Council could reaffirm its common position at the third reading. The proposal was then adopted, unless Parliament rejected it by an absolute majority of its members. Since an absolute majority is difficult to obtain in the European Parliament, the Council's view tended to predominate in the legislative procedure.

The Treaty of Amsterdam has removed the possibility of a third reading in the Council, shortening the procedure. If the two institutions fail to reach a compromise, the proposal is rejected. So in terms of its legislative power, Parliament now stands on an equal footing with the Council, which will have to seek a compromise if it wishes the proposal to be adopted.

A declaration adopted by the intergovernmental conference calls on the institutions concerned (Parliament, the Council and the Commission) to respect the deadlines set by Article 251 (ex Article 189b). The actual period between the second reading by Parliament and the outcome of the Conciliation Committee's deliberations must not exceed nine months.

Future organisation of the European Parliament

The Treaty of Amsterdam limits the size of the European Parliament to 700 members. This figure is not to be exceeded even when the European Union is enlarged to include the countries of central and eastern Europe.

The European Parliament will draw up proposals for elections by direct universal suffrage, in accordance with a uniform procedure in all Member States or in accordance with principles common to all Member States.

With the approval of the Council, and acting by unanimity after consulting the Commission, the European Parliament will lay down regulations governing the performance of its Members' duties.

Parliament's role in the procedure for appointing the members of the Commission has been strengthened through changes to the confirmation procedure introduced by the Treaty of Maastricht. Parliament first has to approve the Member States' choice for President of the Commission before confirming the other members of the Commission nominated by common accord of the Member States in consultation with the President.

A Protocol on the seats of the institutions will be annexed to the various Treaties, confirming the agreement reached at the Edinburgh European Council (December 1992) and stating that the European Parliament is to have its seat 'in Strasbourg where the 12 periods of monthly plenary sessions, including the budget session, shall be held'. Any additional plenary sessions are to be held in Brussels, as are the meetings of the various Parliamentary committees. 'The General Secretariat of the European Parliament and its departments shall remain in Luxembourg.'

INSTITUTIONAL MATTERS

The Council of the European Union

Introduction

A Protocol on the institutions with the prospect of enlargement has been annexed to the EU Treaty and to the Treaties establishing the European Communities. It lays down a number of institutional conditions that will have to be met at the next enlargement and provides for another intergovernmental conference to be convened before the membership of the European Union exceeds 20. The present structure is the legacy of an organisation designed for six Member States and although it has been adjusted to take account of the accession of new members, it still operates today on the same institutional principles.

The Council is facing two main questions:

- weighting of votes of Member States' representatives;
- the scope of qualified majority voting.

The Protocol on the institutions incorporates in a common framework the questions of the weighting of votes in the Council and the size of the Commission, the underlying idea being to revise the Community system so that the relative influence of the small and medium-sized countries should not one day become disproportionate to the size of their population.

The question of the weighting is particularly important owing to the extension of qualified majority voting, since that method of decision-making applies to most of the new provisions introduced by the Treaty of Amsterdam. At the same time, qualified majority voting has also been extended to a number of existing provisions.

The General Secretariat of the Council now also has a special role to play in the context of common foreign and security policy.

Re-weighting of votes and dual majority

Re-weighting of votes or the introduction of a dual majority are two of the options between which the Member States will have to choose before the next enlargement of the European Union. Re-weighting would mean that the proportion of votes allocated to the large countries would be increased in relation to those of the small States. A dual majority, on the other hand, would not, in theory, alter the present weighting but would provide that, for a decision to be adopted within the Council, it would not only have to obtain a number of votes representing a qualified majority, but also correspond to a threshold, yet to be decided on, of the population of the European Union.

The protocol on the institutions links these questions affecting the Council with the reform of the Commission. In practical terms it requires that, on the date of entry into force of the first enlargement, the Commission will comprise one national of each of the Member States, provided that, by that date, the weighting of the votes in the Council has been modified, whether by re-weighting of the votes or by dual majority, in a manner acceptable to all Member States.

Greater use of qualified majority voting

Use of qualified majority voting has been extended to cover the following provisions of the EC Treaty (the article numbers reflect the new numbering):

- the coordination of provisions laid down by law, regulation or administrative action providing for special treatment for foreign nationals (right of establishment, Article 46(2));
- the adoption or amendment of the framework programme for research (Article 166);
- the setting-up of joint undertakings for research and technological development (Articles 171 and 172).

Qualified majority voting also applies to the following new areas introduced into the EC Treaty:

- guidelines on employment (Article 128);
- adoption of incentive measures for employment (Article 129);
- adoption of measures to strengthen customs cooperation between Member States and between them and the Commission (Article 135);
- measures to combat social exclusion (Article 137 (2));
- adoption of measures to ensure the application of the principle of equal opportunities and equal treatment of men and women (Article 141 (3));
- promotion of public health (Article 152 (4));
- the determining of general principles governing the right of access to European Parliament, Council and Commission documents (Article 255);
- measures to combat fraud affecting the financial interests of the Community (Article 280);
- adoption of measures on the establishment of statistics (Article 285);
- establishment of an independent supervisory body responsible for monitoring processing of personal data (Article 286);
- laying down the conditions governing the application of the EC Treaty to the outermost regions (Article 299).

Qualified majority voting is now also used in two cases relating to the common foreign and security policy (Title V of the EU Treaty):

- when adopting decisions implementing a common strategy decided on by the European Council;
- when adopting any decision implementing joint actions or common positions adopted in advance by the Council.

General Secretariat

The Secretary-General of the Council now serves as High Representative for the common foreign and security policy, while the running of the General Secretariat is handled by a Deputy Secretary-General who, like the Secretary-General, is appointed by unanimous Council decision.

The High Representative for the common foreign and security policy assists the Presidency and the Council, in particular by contributing to the formulation, preparation, and implementation of policy decisions. He also fulfils a representative function and is assisted by a policy planning and early warning unit under his responsibility.

INSTITUTIONAL MATTERS

European Commission

Introduction

A protocol on the institutions with the prospect of enlargement has been annexed to the EU Treaty and to the Treaties establishing the European Communities. It lays down a number of institutional conditions that will have to be met at the next enlargement and provides for another intergovernmental conference to be convened before the membership of the European Union exceeds 20. The present structure is the legacy of an organisation designed for six Member States and although it has been adjusted to take account of the accession of new members, it still operates today on the same institutional principles.

Consequently the European Commission is faced with various questions concerning, in particular, its composition, the role of its Presidency and its democratic legitimacy. The Amsterdam Treaty attempts to answer the questions by pursuing the objective of strengthening the institution, of which the main role is to represent the general interests of the Union completely independently.

The new Treaty changes the procedure for confirming the Commission to consolidate its legitimacy along the lines etched out by the Maastricht Treaty. As for the optimum size of the Commission, the Protocol on the institutions has tied this issue to reweighting the votes in the Council.

In addition, in a Declaration to the Final Act, the Intergovernmental Conference called on the Commission to submit to the Council, by the end of 1998, a proposal to amend the procedures for the exercise of implementing powers conferred on the Commission (comitology).

Composition

The composition of the Commission is closely connected to the question of collective responsibility.

This is a distinctive feature of the structure of the Commission and means that decisions adopted by the Commission reflect the views of the full body, rather than the views of individual members. With enlargement, it is feared that a significant increase in the number of Commissioners might increase their responsiveness to national considerations to the detriment of collective responsibility. On the other hand, limiting the number of members is a delicate issue since it would mean that not all nationalities would be represented.

In response to this problem, the Protocol on the institutions provides that at the next enlargement of the Union the Commission will comprise one national of each Member State, provided that by that date the weighting of the votes in the Council has been modified in a manner acceptable to all

Member States. The idea is to revise the scale of weightings so that the relative weight of small and medium-sized countries is not disproportionate to the size of the population.

Presidency

The role of the President of the Commission is to ensure its unity and effectiveness. The Amsterdam Treaty seeks to strengthen the President's position in exercising his function.

The amendment to Article 214 (ex Article 158) strengthens the legitimacy of the President by submitting his nomination for approval by the European Parliament. Under the new provisions, the Members of the Commission are now nominated by common accord with the President, rather than simply after consulting him. Article 219 (ex Article 163) also promotes closer coordination between the Members of the Commission by providing that they 'will work under the political guidance of its President'.

Declaration 32 to the Amsterdam Treaty will also have the effect of strengthening the President's role by providing that he will enjoy broad discretion in the allocation of tasks within the Commission, as well as in any reshuffling of those tasks during a Commission's term of office. The declaration goes on to note the Commission's intention to undertake in parallel a corresponding reorganisation of its departments, and in particular the desirability of bringing external relations under the responsibility of a Vice-President in the interests of consistency.

Right of initiative

The Commission's right of initiative has been strengthened in three ways:

- new provisions will be incorporated in the Treaty establishing the European Community (employment, social affairs, etc.);
- after a transitional period of five years when the right of initiative is shared with the Member States, questions previously covered by Title VI procedures (asylum, immigration, judicial cooperation in civil matters) will come under the Community and the sole right of initiative will pass to the Commission;
- in areas under the third pillar (police and judicial cooperation in criminal matters) the Commission will acquire a shared right of initiative with the Member States.

INSTITUTIONAL MATTERS

The Court of Justice

Introduction

Conferring greater democratic legitimacy on the European institutions is one of the chief aims of the reform of the European Union. The role of the Court of Justice is important in this context since it has the task of ensuring that the law is observed in the interpretation and application of the Treaties, an essential requirement if the European Union is to work along democratic lines.

The Court's powers have been widened by the Treaty of Amsterdam. It now has jurisdiction in areas that previously lay outside its field of competence, but where there is an urgent need to protect individual rights:

- fundamental rights;
- asylum, immigration, free movement of persons and judicial cooperation in civil matters;
- police and judicial cooperation in criminal matters.

Fundamental rights

Article 46 (ex Article L) of the EU Treaty has been amended to extend the powers of the Court of Justice to cover Article 6(2) (ex Article F.2) of the Treaty, as far as action by the European institutions is concerned.

Article 6 requires the Union to respect fundamental rights, as guaranteed by the European Convention on Human Rights. The amendment is important since it formally gives the Court the power to rule on how the Convention is being applied by the Community institutions. This should spur the Court to greater vigilance.

Asylum, immigration, free movement of persons and judicial cooperation in civil matters

A new Title ('Visas, asylum, immigration and other policies related to free movement of persons') has been inserted in the EC Treaty. The Treaty already contained provisions relating to visas (ex Article 100c, which has been repealed). The main changes therefore relate to the new Community framework for questions regarding asylum, immigration, free movement of persons, and judicial cooperation in civil matters.

Under Article 68 the Court now has jurisdiction in the following cases:

- a national court against whose decisions there is no judicial remedy under national law may ask the Court of Justice to give a ruling on a question concerning the interpretation of the new Title or the validity or interpretation of Community acts based on it, if a ruling by the Court is necessary so that the national court can give judgment;

- the Council, the Commission or a Member State may request the Court of Justice to give a ruling on a question of interpretation of the Title or Community acts based on it.

Police and judicial cooperation in criminal matters

Title VI of the EU Treaty has been renamed 'Provisions on police and judicial cooperation in criminal matters'.

Article 35 (ex Article K.7) lays down two restrictions on the Court's powers to rule on matters covered by Title VI:

- preliminary rulings apply only to those Member States which have made a declaration accepting the jurisdiction of the Court (paragraph 2);
- actions for annulment may be brought only by Member States or the Commission (paragraph 6).

The Court also has jurisdiction to rule on any dispute between Member States over the interpretation or application of the measures adopted and on any dispute between Member States and the Commission about the interpretation or application of conventions established under the third pillar.

INSTITUTIONAL MATTERS

The Court of Auditors, the Economic and Social Committee and the Committee of the Regions

The Court of Auditors

The role of the Court of Auditors as a Community institution has been enhanced:

- it is now included in Article 5 (ex Article E) of the EU Treaty;
- it has been given the right to bring actions before the Court of Justice for the purpose of protecting its prerogatives, under Article 230 of the EC Treaty (ex Article 173).

Its powers as a watchdog and investigator have been increased so that more effective steps can be taken to combat fraud to the detriment of the Community budget. It must notify any irregularity in Community revenue or expenditure to the European Parliament and the Council. For this purpose it has been given powers to audit the accounts of external bodies managing Community funds, including the European Investment Bank (EIB).

In the performance of its duties the Court of Auditors may require any relevant documents or information to be produced and may conduct audits 'on the spot in the other institutions of the Community, on the premises of any body which manages revenue or expenditure on behalf of the Community and in the Member States, including on the premises of any natural or legal person in receipt of payments from the budget' (Article 248(3)).

In the case of the EIB, the Court of Auditors has access to the information needed for the audit of Community expenditure and revenue managed by the Bank. Its rights of access will be governed by an agreement between the Court, the Bank and the Commission (such an agreement already existed, and a declaration invites the three institutions concerned to maintain it in force).

In addition to this increase in the powers of the Court of Auditors, Article 248 (ex Article 188c) calls for close cooperation between the Court and national audit bodies.

Furthermore, the statement of assurance provided by the Court as to the reliability of accounts and the legality and regularity of the underlying transactions is to be published in the Official Journal of the European Communities.

The Economic and Social Committee

Consultation of the Economic and Social Committee is mandatory on a wider range of topics. The new areas of the EC Treaty on which the Economic and Social Committee must first be consulted are:

- the guidelines and incentives for employment (Articles 128 and 129);
- the social legislation resulting from the agreements reached by management and labour (Articles 136 to 143);

- implementation of the principle of equal opportunities (Article 141);
- public health (Article 152).

The Economic and Social Committee may also be consulted by the European Parliament if the latter deems such consultation appropriate.

The administrative structure of the Economic and Social Committee is now separate from that of the Committee of the Regions. The Protocol to the EC Treaty providing for a common organisational structure has been repealed.

The Committee of the Regions

The Committee of the Regions must be consulted in the following additional areas:

- the areas listed above for the Economic and Social Committee;
- the environment (Article 175);
- the Social Fund (Article 148);
- vocational training (Article 150);
- cross-border cooperation (first paragraph of Article 265);
- transport (Articles 71 and 80).

The Committee may also be consulted by the European Parliament on other matters.

Like the Economic and Social Committee, the Committee of the Regions now has its own separate administrative structure. Similarly, it may draw up its own rules of procedure without requiring the unanimous approval of the Council, as was required before.

INSTITUTIONAL MATTERS

National parliaments

Introduction

Since 1989 members of the national parliaments and the European Parliament have been meeting at six-monthly intervals within the Conference of European Affairs Committees (COSAC), essentially for the purpose of exchanging information.

When the Treaty of Maastricht came into force, the powers of the European institutions were extended to areas such as justice and home affairs, which had traditionally been national preserves.

It was therefore important that the national parliaments should be kept informed, as fully and as rapidly as possible, so that they (and through them the citizens of the European Union) could be more closely involved in the Community's decision-making process and exercise better control over their country's representatives within the Council.

Given the diversity of their national traditions, the Member States recognised the need to lay down common principles on information for and contributions from the national parliaments. For this reason, a Protocol on the role of national parliaments has been annexed to the founding Treaties.

Parliamentary scrutiny of individual national governments depends on the constitutional practice followed by each Member State. It was considered important, however, to encourage greater involvement of national parliaments in the activities of the European Union and to enhance their ability to express their views on matters which might be of particular interest to them.

Provision of information to the national parliaments of the Members States

The following documents must be promptly forwarded to national parliaments:

- White Papers;
- Green Papers;
- communications;
- proposals for legislation.

The procedure for adopting legislative acts or measures under Title VI of the EU Treaty (police and judicial cooperation in criminal matters) requires there to be at least six weeks between the date when the Commission sends its proposal to the European Parliament and the Council and the date when it is placed on the Council agenda.

This gives national parliaments sufficient time to discuss the proposal, if necessary, with their respective governments.

The Conference of European Affairs Committees (COSAC)

The new Protocol acknowledges the valuable role played by COSAC. The committee can send the EU institutions any contribution it thinks appropriate, especially concerning proposed acts which representatives of the national governments may jointly decide to forward to it in view of the subject matter involved.

Above all, COSAC can examine any legislative proposal concerning the area of freedom, security and justice that might have a direct bearing on the rights and freedoms of individuals. Its observations are forwarded to the European Parliament, the Council and the Commission.

COSAC can also address to the three institutions 'any contribution which it deems appropriate on the legislative activities of the Union, notably in relation to the application of the principle of subsidiarity, the area of freedom, security and justice as well as questions regarding fundamental rights'.

The national parliaments will thus be able to play a larger role in the decision-making process and contribute more to the drafting of EU legislation.

INSTITUTIONAL MATTERS

Subsidiarity

Introduction

One of the major objectives of the Intergovernmental Conference on the revision of the Treaties was to bring the European Union closer to its citizens by enabling them to understand and influence European integration. A number of Community policies, such as those on consumer protection or employment, will be reformed with this specific goal in mind.

Subsidiarity was another major topic of discussion when the conference considered how better to meet the expectations of the people of Europe. To consolidate this principle, on which the efficiency of the European Union depends, a specific protocol has been annexed to the EC Treaty.

Protocol on the principle of subsidiarity

In October 1992, the Birmingham European Council confirmed that decisions should be taken as closely as possible to the citizens of the Union in accordance with Article 5 (ex Article 3b) of the EC Treaty.

With this in mind, the Edinburgh European Council of December 1992 agreed an overall approach for applying the principle of subsidiarity (basic principles, guidelines, and procedures).

The protocol on the application of the principles of subsidiarity and proportionality codifies the guidelines adopted by the Edinburgh European Council and gives them force in law. By this means the Member States intend to formalise a number of aspects relating to subsidiarity:

- subsidiarity is a dynamic concept and the appropriate level for action may vary according to circumstances;
- all legislative proposals will be accompanied by a statement on the impact of the proposed measure on the application of the principle of subsidiarity;
- consistent with the proper achievement of the objective, the form of Community action should not be too restrictive (as far as possible, directives should be preferred to regulations);
- subsidiarity should not undermine the powers conferred on the European Community by the Treaty, as interpreted by the Court of Justice.

The main condition for embarking on Community action is set out in the second paragraph of Article 5 of the EC Treaty, which states that the Community shall take action 'only if and in so far as the objectives of the proposed action cannot be sufficiently achieved by the Member States and can therefore, by reason of the scale or effects of the proposed action, be better achieved by the Community'.

The Protocol cites three criteria for judging whether this condition has been fulfilled:

- does the action have transnational aspects that cannot be satisfactorily regulated by the Member States?
- would action by Member States or lack of action conflict with the requirements of the Treaty?
- would action at Community level produce clear benefits?

INSTITUTIONAL MATTERS

Closer cooperation

Introduction

The future enlargement of the European Union to central and eastern Europe means that it will be essential to review how the European institutions work. The current structure is inherited from an organisation designed for six Member States and, although it has undergone adjustments to take the accession of new Member States into account, it still works on the same institutional principles.

The increase in the number of Member States will increase diversity within the European Union in terms of each Member State's objectives, sensibilities and priorities. While this diversity is what constitutes the wealth of the European Union, it may also be an obstacle, if the pace of European integration is determined by the slowest.

The Treaty of Amsterdam represents an unprecedented reform, since it introduces the concept of variable-speed integration into the EU Treaty. In concrete terms, three articles have been added to the EU Treaty (Articles 43 to 45). They allow Member States that intend to establish closer cooperation between one another to make use of the institutions, procedures, and mechanisms laid down by the EU Treaty and the EC Treaty.

Closer cooperation enables the most ambitious Member States to deepen cooperation between themselves while leaving the door open to other Member States to join them at a later stage.

Conditions

The Treaty of Amsterdam stipulates a number of general conditions that must be met before closer cooperation can be launched. These are necessary to ensure that the initiative does not jeopardise the functioning of the internal market. In other words, the Community *acquis* must be preserved. Therefore, before any closer cooperation can be launched, it must show that it will:

- aim to further the objectives of the Union and protect and serve its interests;
- respect the principles of the Treaties and the single institutional framework of the Union;
- be used only as a last resort;
- concern at least a majority of Member States;
- not affect the Community *acquis* or the measures adopted under the other provisions of the Treaties;
- not affect the competences, rights, obligations and interests of those Member States which do not participate in it;

- be open to all Member States and allow them to become parties to the cooperation at any time, provided that they comply with the basic decision and with the decisions taken within that framework.

Closer cooperation is possible in the fields covered by the EC Treaty and in police and judicial cooperation in criminal matters. As far as the common foreign and security policy (CFSP) is concerned, the authors of the Treaty of Amsterdam decided that constructive abstention was already designed to meet flexibility requirements, and that recourse to closer cooperation was therefore unnecessary.

Depending on the pillar concerned, closer cooperation will have to meet certain specific conditions in addition to the general conditions set out in Article K.15.

- For the first pillar, the cooperation envisaged:
  - must not concern areas which fall within the exclusive competence of the Community;
  - must not affect Community policies, actions or programmes;
  - must not concern the citizenship of the Union or discriminate between nationals of Member States;
  - must remain within the limits of the powers conferred upon the Community by the Treaty;
  - must not constitute a discrimination or a restriction of trade between Member States and will not distort the conditions of competition between them.
- For the third pillar, the cooperation envisaged:
  - must respect the powers of the European Community and the objectives laid down by Title VI of the Treaty on European Union;
  - must have the aim of enabling the Union to develop more rapidly into an area of freedom, security and justice.

Activation

A new Article 11 has been inserted in the EC Treaty.

This new article provides that, within the framework of the European Community, the initiative for closer cooperation must come from the European Commission following a request to this end by the Member States concerned. The Commission is free to submit a proposal, but if it decides not to do so, it must inform the Member States concerned of the reasons.

When the Council receives a proposal for closer cooperation from the Commission, it must act by qualified majority after consulting the European Parliament.

For the field of police and judicial cooperation in criminal matters (third pillar), the procedure differs from that used within the framework of the European Community. The new Article 40 of the EU Treaty provides that the initiative for closer cooperation must come from the Member States concerned. Activation is therefore subject to a Council decision by qualified majority. The Commission is asked for its opinion and the Member States' request is transmitted to the European Parliament.

Safeguard clause

In both the first and third pillars, launching closer cooperation depends on a decision taken by a qualified majority of the Council.

However, the Member States have a safeguard clause allowing any of them to prevent a vote being taken for important reasons of national policy.

The Council, acting by qualified majority, can then send the question to the European Council if the decision falls under the third pillar, or to the Council, in the shape of the Heads of State or Government, if the decision falls under the first pillar. In both cases, referral requires a unanimous decision.

In this case, the role of the Court of Justice is crucial because it will have to decide on the degree of importance of the reasons of national policy invoked by a Member State. The Court of Justice therefore acts as a guarantee that the safeguard clause is not abused.

Operation

For the implementation of closer cooperation, the new Article 44 of the EU Treaty provides that all members of the Council may take part in the deliberations, but that only those representing Member States participating in closer cooperation play a part in adopting decisions.

Any closer cooperation is subject to all the relevant provisions of whichever Treaty it falls under (EU Treaty or EC Treaty). Depending on the subject, decisions are taken under the procedure laid down for the field in question (unanimity, qualified majority vote, co-decision or consultation procedures, etc.).

A qualified majority is defined as the same proportion of the weighted votes of the members of the Council concerned as laid down in Article 205(2) (ex Article 148(2)) of the EC Treaty.

It should also be noted that the other institutions involved in the decision-making process (notably the European Parliament and the Commission) do so in their entirety, making no distinction between Member States which are taking part in closer cooperation and those which are not.

Subsequent participation by a Member State

The basic principle underlying the system is that participation in closer cooperation is open to any Member State, including those that are not involved from the start.

In the Community field, a Member State wishing to join the others must inform the Council and the Commission of its intention. The Commission then delivers its opinion to the Council within three months. A month after giving its opinion, the Commission decides on the matter and on any specific arrangements it considers necessary.

For closer cooperation under the third pillar, the procedure is different from that under the first pillar, although the time limits specified are the same. In addition to its opinion, the Commission may give a recommendation on specific provisions it considers necessary for the Member State to take part in the cooperation in question. It is then for the Council to take the decision. The request is approved unless the Council decides, by qualified majority, to hold it in abeyance. In this case, the Council must give its reasons and set a deadline for the request to be re-examined.

Financing

Except for administrative costs, the expenditure arising from closer cooperation is borne by the participating Member States, unless the Council unanimously decides otherwise.

INSTITUTIONAL MATTERS

Decision-making procedures

Introduction

Decision-making in the European Union comprises several different procedures. This means that the different institutions play different roles depending on the subject matter concerned. As a rule, decision-making principally involves three institutions: the European Parliament, the Council and the Commission. However, other institutions and bodies such as the Court of Auditors, the European Central Bank, the Economic and Financial Committee, the Economic and Social Committee and the Committee of the Regions also play a role in certain specific areas. The various bodies operate within the powers conferred on them by the Treaties.

The description below covers the provisions of both the EU Treaty and the EC Treaty. It is organised by subject, following the title and chapter headings in the Treaties. ***Bold italics*** indicate changes introduced by the Amsterdam Treaty, whether in the form of a new provision or the amendment of a decision-making procedure.

Treaty on European Union

1. Human rights and fundamental freedoms

Determining the existence of a serious and persistent breach of the principles on which the European Union is founded ***(Article 7(1)):***

- proposal by one third of the Member States or the Commission — assent of the European Parliament acting by a two-thirds majority of the votes cast, representing a majority of its members — Council, meeting in the composition of the Heads of State or Government, acting by unanimity (disregarding the vote of the Member State in question).

Decision to suspend certain rights deriving from the application of the Treaty to the Member State in question ***(Article 7(2)):***

- Council acting by a qualified majority (disregarding the vote of the Member State in question).

Decision to revoke or vary suspension measures taken against a Member State ***(Article 7(3)):***

- Council acting by a qualified majority (disregarding the vote of the Member State in question).

2. Common foreign and security policy (CFSP)

Adopting common strategies and setting out their objectives, duration and the means to be made available by the Union and the

Member States for their implementation ***(Article 13):***

- decision by European Council.

Decisions under the common foreign and security policy ***(Article 23(1))***:

- Council acting unanimously (abstention by a Member State not preventing the adoption of such decisions).

Adopting joint actions and common positions on the basis of a common strategy ***(Article 23(2), first subparagraph, first indent):***

- Council acting by a qualified majority (with at least 10 members voting in favour).

Adopting any decision implementing a joint action or a common position ***(Article 23(2), first subparagraph, second indent):***

- Council acting by a qualified majority (with at least 10 members voting in favour).

Referring a decision to the European Council where a member of the Council declares that, for important reasons of national policy, it opposes the adoption of a decision to be taken by qualified majority ***(Article 23(2), second subparagraph):***

- Council acting by a qualified majority (with at least 10 members voting in favour).

Procedure for concluding an agreement with one or more States or international organisations ***(Article 24):***

- Council, acting unanimously, may authorise the Presidency, assisted by the Commission, to open negotiations — recommendation from the Presidency — agreement concluded by the Council acting unanimously.

Decision not to charge certain expenditure to the budget of the European Communities ***(Article 28):***

- Council acting unanimously.

3. Police and judicial cooperation in criminal matters

Adoption of common positions, ***framework decisions*** and ***decisions (Article 34(2)(a), (b) and (c)):***

- ***initiative of Commission*** or a Member State — Council acting unanimously.

Adoption of measures necessary for implementing a decision ***(Article 34(2)(c)):***

- Council acting by a qualified majority (with at least 10 members voting in favour).

Adoption of conventions (Article 34(2)(d), first subparagraph, ex Article K.3):

- ***initiative of Commission*** or a Member State — Council acting unanimously — ratification by Member States in accordance with their respective constitutional requirements — ***conventions, once adopted by at least half of the Member States, enter into force for those Member States.***

Adoption of measures implementing conventions (Article 34(2)(d), second subparagraph, ex Article K.6):

- within the Council by a majority of two-thirds of the contracting parties.

Establishing closer cooperation under Title VI ***(Article 40(2), first subparagraph):***

- at request of Member States concerned — Commission consulted — Council acting by a qualified majority (with at least 10 members voting in favour).

Referring a decision to the European Council where a member of the Council declares that, for important reasons of national policy, it opposes the granting of authorisation for closer cooperation ***(Article 40(2), second subparagraph):***

- Council acting by a qualified majority (with at least 10 members voting in favour).

Decision not to charge certain expenditure to the budget of the European Communities ***(Article 41):***

- Council acting unanimously.

Transferring action in areas covered by Title VI of the Treaty on European Union to Title IV of the Treaty establishing the European Community (Article 42, ex Article K.14):

- initiative of Commission or a Member State — European Parliament consulted — Council acting unanimously — ratification by Member States in accordance with their respective constitutional requirements.

4. Final provisions

Amending the Treaties on which the European Union is founded (Article 48, ex Article N):

- proposal from a Member State or the Commission — European Parliament and, where appropriate, Commission consulted (Council and European Central Bank also consulted where changes relate to the monetary area) — Council opinion in favour — conference of representatives of governments of Member States convened by President of Council to determine by common accord the amendments to be made to the Treaties — ratification by Member States in accordance with their respective constitutional requirements.

Accession to the European Union by a European State (Article 49, ex Article O):

- application from prospective member — Commission consulted — assent of European Parliament — Council acting unanimously — ratification by all the contracting States in accordance with their respective constitutional requirements.

Treaty establishing the European Community

1. Closer cooperation

Authorisation to establish closer cooperation ***(Article 11(2), first subparagraph):***

- Commission proposal — European Parliament consulted — Council acting by a qualified majority.

Referral to the Council, meeting in the composition of the Heads of State or Government, where a Member State declares that, for important reasons of national policy, it opposes the granting of authorisation for closer cooperation ***(Article 11(2), second subparagraph):***

- Council acting by a qualified majority (with at least 10 members voting in favour).

Authorisation to establish closer cooperation granted by the Council, meeting in the composition of the Heads of State or Government ***(Article 11(2), second subparagraph):***

- Council acting unanimously.

2. Discrimination on grounds of nationality

Adopting rules to prohibit such discrimination (Article 12, ex Article 6):

- ***co-decision procedure.***

3. Discrimination based on sex, racial or ethnic origin, religion or belief, disability, age or sexual orientation

Measures necessary to combat all forms of discrimination ***(Article 13):***

- Commission proposal — European Parliament consulted — Council acting unanimously.

4. Establishing the single market (see also points 6, 8, 9, 10, 11 and 16)

Determining the guidelines and conditions necessary to ensure balanced progress in all the sectors covered by the four freedoms (Article 14(3), ex Article 7 A):

- Commission proposal — Council acting by a qualified majority.

5. Citizenship of the Union

Adopting provisions to facilitate the exercise of Union citizenship rights (Article 18, ex Article 8 A):

- ***co–decision procedure*** with the Council acting unanimously.

Arrangements for exercising the right to vote and to stand as a candidate in municipal elections (Article 19(1), ex Article 8 B):

- Commission proposal — European Parliament consulted — Council acting unanimously.

Arrangements for exercising the right to vote and to stand as a candidate in elections to the European Parliament (Article 19(2), ex Article 8 B):

- Commission proposal — European Parliament consulted — Council acting unanimously.

Provisions to strengthen or add to the Union citizenship rights (Article 22, ex Article 8 E):

- Commission proposal — European Parliament consulted — Council acting unanimously.

6. Free movement of goods

Fixing Common Customs Tariff duties (Article 26, ex Article 28):

- Commission proposal — Council acting by a qualified majority.

7. Agriculture

Adopting regulations, directives, decisions and common market organisation arrangements (Article 37(2) and (3), ex Article 43):

- Commission proposal — European Parliament consulted — Council acting by a qualified majority.

8. Free movement of workers

Adopting measures to bring about freedom of movement for workers (Article 40, ex Article 49):

- co-decision procedure with Economic and Social Committee consulted.

Adopting measures in the field of social security to provide freedom of movement for workers (Article 42, ex Article 51):

- ***co-decision procedure*** with the Council acting unanimously.

9. Right of establishment

Issuing directives to bring about freedom of establishment (Article 44, ex Article 54):

- co-decision procedure with Economic and Social Committee consulted.

Exempting certain activities from the provisions of the 'Right of establishment' Chapter (Article 45, ex Article 55):

- Commission proposal — Council acting by a qualified majority.

Directives on coordinating provisions laying down special treatment of foreign nationals on grounds of public policy, public security or public health (Article 46, ex Article 56):

- co-decision procedure.

Directives for the mutual recognition of diplomas, certificates and other evidence of formal qualifications (Article 47(1), ex Article 57):

- co-decision procedure.

Directives for the coordination of provisions laid down by law, regulation or administrative action in Member States concerning the taking-up and pursuit of activities as self-employed persons (Article 47(2), ex Article 57):

- co-decision procedure (with the Council acting unanimously, where implementing the directive requires amendments to be made in at least one Member State to the existing legal principles governing training and conditions of access for natural persons to professions).

10. Services

Extending the provisions of the 'Services' Chapter to service providers who are nationals of a third country, but established within the Community (Article 49, ex Article 59):

- Commission proposal — Council acting by a qualified majority.

Directives to liberalise a specific service (Article 52, ex Article 63):

- Commission proposal — Economic and Social Committee consulted — Council acting by a qualified majority.

11. Capital and payments

Measures on the movement of capital to or from third countries involving direct investment — including investment in real estate — establishment, the provision of financial services or the admission of securities to capital markets (Article 57, ex Article 73 C):

- Commission proposal — Council acting by a qualified majority (unanimity required for measures constituting a step back in Community law as regards the liberalisation of the movement of capital).

Safeguard measures where, in exceptional circumstances, movements of capital to or from third countries cause, or threaten to cause, serious difficulties for the operation of economic and monetary union (Article 59, ex Article 73 F):

- Commission proposal — European Central Bank consulted — Council acting by a qualified majority.

Urgent measures to suspend or reduce economic relations between the European Union and a third country (Article 60(1), ex Article 73 G):

- Commission proposal — Council acting by a qualified majority.

Amending or abolishing unilateral measures taken by a Member State against a third country (Article 60(2), ex Article 73 G):

- Commission proposal — Council acting by a qualified majority.

12. Visas, asylum, immigration and other policies related to free movement of persons

Measures to ensure the absence of any controls on persons, when crossing internal borders ***(Article 62(1)):***

- Commission proposal or initiative of a Member State — European Parliament consulted — Council acting unanimously (for a transitional period of five years after the entry into force of the Treaty of Amsterdam)/Commission proposal — Council acting unanimously to make a decision about the required procedure (after the transitional period).

Measures on standards and procedures to be followed by Member States in carrying out checks on persons at external borders ***(Article 62(2)(a)):***

- Commission proposal or initiative of a Member State — European Parliament consulted — Council acting unanimously (for a transitional period of five years after the entry into force of the Treaty of Amsterdam)/Commission proposal — Council acting unanimously to make a decision about the required procedure (after the transitional period).

Adoption of a uniform format for visas and a list of third countries whose nationals must be in possession of visas when crossing the external borders ***(Article 62(2)(b)(i) and (iii)):***

- Commission proposal — European Parliament consulted — Council acting by a qualified majority.

Establishing the procedures and conditions for issuing visas by Member States and rules on a uniform visa ***(Article 62(2)(b)(ii) and (iv)):***

- Commission proposal or initiative of a Member State — European Parliament consulted — Council acting unanimously (for a transitional period of five years after the entry into force of the Treaty of Amsterdam)/co-decision (after the transitional period).

Measures setting out the conditions under which nationals of third countries shall have the freedom to travel within the territory of the Member States during a period of no more than three months ***(Article 62(3)):***

- Commission proposal or initiative of a Member State — European Parliament consulted — Council acting unanimously (for a transitional period of five years after the entry into force of the Treaty of Amsterdam)/Commission proposal — Council acting unanimously to make a decision about the required procedure (after the transitional period).

Measures on asylum (criteria and mechanisms for determining which Member State is responsible for considering an application for asylum, minimum standards on the reception of asylum seekers, conditions for qualifying for refugee status, for granting or withdrawing refugee status) ***(Article 63(1)):***

- Commission proposal or initiative of a Member State — European Parliament consulted — Council acting unanimously (for a transitional period of five years after the entry into force of the Treaty of Amsterdam)/Commission proposal — Council acting unanimously to make a decision about the required procedure (after the transitional period).

Measures on refugees and displaced persons (granting temporary protection) ***(Article 63(2)(a)):***

- Commission proposal or initiative of a Member State — European Parliament consulted — Council acting unanimously (for a transitional period of five years after the entry into force of the Treaty of

Amsterdam)/Commission proposal — Council acting unanimously to make a decision about the required procedure (after the transitional period).

Measures on refugees and displaced persons (balance of effort between Member States) ***(Article 63(2)(b)):***

- Commission proposal or initiative of a Member State — European Parliament consulted — Council acting unanimously.

Measures on immigration policy (conditions of entry and residence, and standards on procedures for issuing long-term visas and residence permits) ***(Article 63(3)(a)):***

- Commission proposal or initiative of a Member State — European Parliament consulted — Council acting unanimously.

Measures on immigration policy (illegal immigration and illegal residence) ***(Article 63(3)(b)):***

- Commission proposal or initiative of a Member State — European Parliament consulted — Council acting unanimously (for a transitional period of five years after the entry into force of the Treaty of Amsterdam)/Commission proposal — Council acting unanimously to make a decision about the required procedure (after the transitional period).

Measures defining the rights and conditions under which nationals of third countries who are legally resident in a Member State may reside in other Member States ***(Article 63(4)):***

- Commission proposal or initiative of a Member State — European Parliament consulted — Council acting unanimously.

Provisional measures in an emergency situation characterised by a sudden inflow of nationals of third countries ***(Article 64):***

- Commission proposal — Council acting by a qualified majority.

Measures in the field of judicial cooperation in civil matters having cross-border implications ***(Article 65):***

- Commission proposal or initiative of a Member State — European Parliament consulted — Council acting unanimously (for a transitional period of five years after the entry into force of the Treaty of Amsterdam)/Commission proposal — Council acting unanimously to make a decision about the required procedure (after the transitional period).

Measures to ensure cooperation between the relevant departments of the administrations of the Member States, as well as between those departments and the Commission ***(Article 66):***

- Commission proposal or initiative of a Member State — European Parliament consulted — Council acting unanimously (for a transitional period of five years after the entry into force of the Treaty of Amsterdam)/Commission proposal — Council acting unanimously to make a decision about the required procedure (after the transitional period).

Decision to provide for all or parts of the areas covered by Title IV to be governed by the co-decision procedure after the end of the transitional period and to adapt the provisions relating to the powers of the Court of Justice ***(Article 67(2), second indent):***

- European Parliament consulted — Council acting unanimously.

13. Transport

Common rules, conditions under which non-resident carriers may operate transport services within a Member State, safety and other appropriate provisions (Article 71(1), ex Article 75):

- ***co-decision procedure*** with Economic and Social Committee and ***Committee of the Regions*** consulted.

Provisions concerning the principles of the regulatory system for transport, the application of which would be liable to have a serious effect on the standard of living and on employment in certain areas and on the operation of transport facilities (Article 71(2), ex Article 75):

- Commission proposal — European Parliament and Economic and Social Committee consulted — Council acting unanimously.

Rules to abolish discrimination which takes the form of carriers charging different rates and imposing different conditions (Article 75, ex Article 79):

- Commission proposal — Economic and Social Committee consulted — Council acting by a qualified majority.

Deciding whether, to what extent and by what procedure appropriate provisions may be laid down for sea and air transport (Article 80, ex Article 84):

- Council acting by a qualified majority.

14. Rules on competition

Adopting appropriate regulations or directives to give effect to the principles set out in Articles 81 and 82 (Article 83, ex Article 87):

- Commission proposal — European Parliament consulted — Council acting by a qualified majority.

Derogation whereby State aid that would normally be in breach of Community law is, in exceptional circumstances, considered to be compatible with the common market:

- Request by a Member State — Council acting unanimously.

Adopting appropriate regulations for the application of Articles 87 and 88 in respect of State aid (Article 89, ex Article 94):

- Commission proposal — European Parliament consulted — Council acting by a qualified majority.

15. Tax provisions

Remissions and repayments for a limited period in respect of exports to other Member States (Article 92, ex Article 98):

- Commission proposal — Council acting by a qualified majority.

Harmonisation of legislation concerning turnover taxes, excise duties and other forms of indirect taxation (Article 93, ex Article 99):

- Commission proposal — European Parliament and Economic and Social Committee consulted — Council acting unanimously.

16. Approximation of laws

Issuing directives for the approximation of such laws, regulations or administrative provisions of the Member States as directly affect the common market (Article 94, ex Article 100):

- Commission proposal — European Parliament and Economic and Social Committee consulted — Council acting unanimously.

Establishment and functioning of the internal market (Article 95, ex Article 100A):

- co-decision procedure with Economic and Social Committee consulted.

Special cases where distortion of competition needs to be eliminated (Article 96, ex Article 101):

- Commission proposal — Council acting by a qualified majority.

17. Economic policy

Adopting recommendations setting out broad economic policy guidelines (Article 99(2), ex Article 103):

- Commission recommendation — draft adopted by the Council acting by a qualified majority — report to European Council — conclusion of European Council — on basis of European Council conclusion, recommendation adopted by Council acting by qualified majority.

Recommendations to Member States acting inconsistently with the broad economic policy guidelines (Article 99(4), ex Article 103):

- Commission recommendation — Council acting by a qualified majority.

Decision to make Council recommendations public (Article 99(4), ex Article 103):

- Commission proposal — Council acting by a qualified majority.

Possibility of adopting detailed rules for the multilateral surveillance procedure in respect of economic policies (Article 99(5), ex Article 103):

- cooperation procedure.

Appropriate measures in the event of severe difficulties arising in the supply of certain products (Article 100(1), ex Article 103 A):

- Commission proposal — Council acting unanimously.

Community financial assistance for a Member State in difficulties caused by exceptional occurrences beyond its control (Article 100(2), ex Article 103 A):

- Commission proposal — Council acting unanimously (qualified majority where the severe difficulties are cause by natural disasters).

Application of the prohibition on assuming commitments and providing overdraft facilities (Article 103, ex Article 104 B):

- cooperation procedure.

Establishing the existence of an excessive deficit (Article 104(6), ex Article 104 C):

- Commission recommendation — Council acting by a qualified majority.

Excessive deficit procedure (Article 104(7)–(9), (11) and (12), ex Article 104 C):

- Commission recommendation — Council acting by a majority of two thirds of the weighted votes of its members, excluding the votes of the representative of the Member State concerned.

Amending the Protocol on the excessive deficit procedure (Article 104(14), ex Article 104 C):

- Commission proposal — European Parliament and European Central Bank consulted — Council acting unanimously.

18. Monetary policy

Decision conferring upon the ECB specific tasks concerning policies relating to the prudential supervision of credit institutions and other financial institutions with the exception of insurance undertakings (Article 105):

- Commission proposal — European Central Bank consulted — assent of European Parliament — Council acting unanimously.

Measures to harmonise the denominations and technical specifications of all coins intended for circulation in the Community (Article 106, ex Article 105 A):

- cooperation procedure with European Central Bank consulted.

Amending the Statute of the European System of Central Banks (ESCB) (Article 107(5), ex Article 106):

- either: recommendation from European Central Bank — Commission consulted — assent of European Parliament — Council acting by a qualified majority;
- or: Commission proposal — European Central Bank consulted — assent of European Parliament — Council acting unanimously.

Adoption of certain provisions referred to in the Statute of the European System of Central Banks (ESCB) (Article 107(6), ex Article 107):

- either: Commission proposal — European Parliament and European Central Bank consulted — Council acting by a qualified majority;
- or: recommendation from European Central Bank — Commission and European Parliament consulted — Council acting by a qualified majority.

Conclusion of formal agreements on an exchange-rate system for the euro in relation to non-Community currencies (Article 111(1), ex Article 109):

- Commission or European Central Bank recommendation — Council acting unanimously.

Adopting, adjusting or abandoning the central rates of the euro (Article 111(1), ex Article 109):

- either: recommendation from European Central Bank — Council acting by a qualified majority;
- or: Commission recommendation — European Central Bank consulted — Council acting by a qualified majority.

Formulating general orientations in the absence of an exchange-rate system in relation to one or more non-Community currencies (Article 111(2), ex Article 109):

- either: recommendation from European Central Bank — Council acting by a qualified majority;
- or: Commission recommendation — European Central Bank consulted — Council acting by a qualified majority.

Arrangements for negotiating and concluding agreements concerning monetary or foreign exchange regime matters (Article 111(3), ex Article 109):

- Commission recommendation — European Central Bank consulted — Council acting by a qualified majority.

19. Institutional provisions in the area of economic and monetary policy

Adopting detailed rules on the make-up of the Economic and Financial Committee (Article 114, ex Article 109 C):

- Commission proposal — European Central Bank and Economic and Financial Committee consulted — Council acting by a qualified majority.

20. Transitional provisions in the area of economic and monetary policy

Ending derogations for Member States unable to adopt the single currency (Greece and Sweden) from the outset of the third phase (Article 122, ex Article 109 K):

- Commission proposal — European Parliament consulted — Council, meeting in the composition of the Heads of State or Government, by qualified majority.

Adoption, on 1 January 1999, of the conversion rates at which the national currencies shall be irrevocably fixed and at which irrevocably fixed rate the ECU shall be substituted for these currencies (Article 123, ex Article 109 L):

- Commission proposal — European Central Bank consulted — Council acting with the unanimity of those Member States not subject to a derogation.

21. Employment

Drawing up guidelines for the Member States to take into account in their employment policies ***(Article 128(2)):***

- conclusions of European Council — Commission proposal — European Parliament, Economic and Social Committee, Committee of the Regions and Employment Committee consulted — Council acting by a qualified majority.

Recommendations to Member States concerning employment policy ***(Article 128(4))***:

- Commission recommendation — Council acting by a qualified majority.

Adoption of incentive measures designed to encourage cooperation between Member States and to support their action in the field of employment ***(Article 129)***:

- co-decision procedure with Economic and Social Committee and Committee of the Regions consulted.

22. Common commercial policy

Adopting directives to harmonise the systems for granting aid for exports to third countries (Article 132, ex Article 112):

- Commission proposal — Council acting by a qualified majority.

Exercising the powers conferred on the Council under Article 133 (Article 133, ex Article 113):

- Qualified majority.

Extending Article 133 to international negotiations and agreements on services and intellectual property (Article 133(5), ex Article 113):

- Commission proposal — European Parliament consulted — Council acting unanimously.

23. Customs cooperation

Measures to strengthen customs cooperation between Member States and between the latter and the Commission ***(Article 135):***

- co-decision procedure

24. Social provisions

Adoption of directives laying down minimum requirements in the social field and measures designed to encourage cooperation between Member States (Article 137***(2)***, ex Article 118):

- co-decision procedure with Economic and Social Committee and Committee of the Regions consulted.

Adoption of measures concerning social security and social protection of workers, protection of workers where their employment contract is terminated, representation and collective defence of the interests of workers and employers, including co-determination, subject to paragraph 6, conditions of employment for third-country nationals legally residing in Community territory and financial contributions for promotion of employment and job creation, without prejudice to the provisions relating to the Social Fund. (Article 137***(3)***, ex Article 118):

- Commission proposal — European Parliament, Economic and Social Committee and Committee of the Regions consulted — Council acting unanimously.

Decisions on implementing Community-level agreements between labour and management (Article 139***(2)***, ex Article 118 B):

- Commission proposal — Council acting by a qualified majority (unanimity where the decisions concerns one of the areas in Article 137(3)).

Adoption of measures to ensure the application of the principle of equal opportunities and equal treatment of men and women in matters of employment and occupation (Article 141***(3)***, ex Article 119):

- co-decision procedure with Economic and Social Committee consulted.

Assigning to the Commission tasks in connection with the implementation of common measures, particularly as regards social security for the migrant workers (Article 144, ex Article 121):

- Council acting unanimously after consultation of Economic and Social Committee.

25. European Social Fund

Adoption of implementing decisions relating to the European Social Fund (Article 148, ex Article 125):

- ***co–decision procedure*** with Economic and Social Committee and ***the Committee of the Regions*** consulted.

26. Education, vocational training and youth

Adoption of incentive measures to contribute to the achievement of the Community's objectives in the field of education (Article 149(4), first indent, ex Article 126):

- co-decision procedure with Economic and Social Committee and the Committee of the Regions consulted.

Adoption of recommendations to contribute to the achievement of the Community's objectives in the field of education (Article 149(4), second indent, ex Article 126):

- Commission proposal — Council acting by a qualified majority.

Adoption of measures to contribute to the achievement of the Community's objectives in the field of vocational training (Article 150, ex Article 127):

- ***co-decision procedure*** with Economic and Social Committee and ***the Committee of the Regions*** consulted.

27. Culture

Adoption of incentive measures to contribute to the achievement of the Community's objectives in the field of culture (Article 151(5), first indent, ex Article 128):

- co-decision procedure with Committee of the Regions consulted (Council acting unanimously throughout procedure).

Adoption of recommendations to contribute to the achievement of the Community's objectives in the field of culture (Article 151(5), second indent, ex Article 128):

- Commission proposal — Council acting unanimously.

28. Public health

Adoption of measures and incentive measures to contribute to the achievement of the Community's objectives in the field of public health ***(including the veterinary and plant health areas)*** (Article 152***(4)***, ex Article 129):

- co-decision procedure with Economic and Social Committee and Committee of the Regions consulted.

Adoption of recommendations to contribute to the achievement of the Community's objectives in the field of public health (Article 152, ex Article 129):

- Commission proposal — Council acting by a qualified majority.

29. Consumer protection

Adoption of measures which support, supplement and monitor the policy pursued by the Member States (Article 153***(4)***, ex Article 129 A):

- co-decision procedure with Economic and Social Committee consulted.

30. Trans-European networks

Adoption of guidelines and measures to achieve the Community's objectives in the field of trans-European networks (Article 156, ex Article 129 D):

- ***co-decision*** procedure with Economic and Social Committee and Committee of the Regions consulted (guidelines and projects of common interest which relate to the territory of a Member State require the approval of the Member State concerned).

31. Industry

Adoption of special measures to support action by the Member States to achieve the objectives of the Community and the Member States in the field of industry (Article 157, ex Article 130):

- Commission proposal — European Parliament and Economic and Social Committee consulted — Council acting unanimously.

32. Economic and social cohesion

Specific action proving necessary outside the Funds (Article 159, ex Article 130 B):

- Commission proposal — European Parliament, Economic and Social Committee and Committee of the Regions consulted — Council acting unanimously.

Defining the tasks, priority objectives and the organisation of the Structural Funds, as well as the general rules applicable to them and the provisions necessary to ensure their effectiveness and their coordination with one another and with the other existing financial instruments (Article 161, ex Article 130 D):

- Commission proposal — assent of European Parliament — Economic and Social Committee and Committee of the Regions consulted — Council acting unanimously.

Implementing decisions relating to the European Regional Development Fund (Article 162, ex Article 130 E):

- ***co-decision procedure*** with Economic and Social Committee and Committee of the Regions consulted.

33. Research and technological development

Adoption of multiannual framework programme (Article 166(1), ex Article 130 I):

- co-decision procedure after Economic and Social Committee consulted ***(Council acting by qualified majority throughout procedure).***

Adoption of specific programmes implementing the multiannual framework programme (Article 166(4), ex Article 130 I):

- Commission proposal — European Parliament and Economic and Social Committee consulted — Council acting by a qualified majority.

Negotiation and conclusion of research and technological development agreements with third countries and international organisations (Article 170, ex Article 130 M):

- Article 300 procedure (ex Article 228): Commission recommendations to Council — Council authorises Commission to open and conduct the necessary negotiations in conjunction with the special committees appointed by the Council and in line with directives fixed by the Council — agreement concluded by Council (by qualified majority or unanimously depending on procedure required for the adoption of internal rules).

Setting up joint undertakings or any other structure necessary for the efficient execution of Community research, technological development and demonstration programmes (Article 172, first paragraph, ex Article 130 O):

- Commission proposal — European Parliament and Economic and Social Committee consulted — Council acting ***by a qualified majority.***

Decisions on detailed rules implementing the multiannual framework programme and the rules applicable to the supplementary programmes (Article 172, second paragraph, ex Article 130 O):

- ***co-decision procedure*** with Economic and Social Committee consulted (adoption of supplementary programmes requires agreement of Member States concerned).

34. Environment

Negotiation and conclusion of agreements between the Community and third countries or international organisations (Article 174, ex Article 130 R):

- Article 300 procedure (ex Article 228): Commission recommendations to Council — Council authorises Commission to open and conduct the necessary negotiations in conjunction with the special committees appointed by the Council and in line with directives fixed by the Council — agreement concluded by Council (by qualified majority or unanimously depending on procedure required for the adoption of internal rules).

Action to be taken to achieve the Community's environmental objectives (Article 175(1), ex Article 130 S):

- ***co-decision procedure*** with Economic and Social Committee ***and Committee of the Regions consulted.***

Adoption, by way of derogation from Article 175(1), of fiscal provisions, measures concerning town and country planning, land use, management of water resources and energy supply. (Article 175(2), first subparagraph, ex Article 130 S):

- Commission proposal — European Parliament, Economic and Social Committee ***and Committee of the Regions*** consulted — Council acting unanimously.

Definition of matters referred to in Article 175(2), where decisions must be taken by qualified majority (Article 175(2), second subparagraph, ex Article 130 S):

- Commission proposal — European Parliament, Economic and Social Committee ***and Committee of the Regions*** consulted — Council acting unanimously.

Adoption of general action programmes setting out priority objectives to be attained (Article 175(3), ex Article 130 S):

- co-decision procedure with Economic and Social Committee ***and Committee of the Regions*** consulted.

Implementation of action programmes referred to in Article 175(3) (Article 175(4), ex Article 130 S):

- as appropriate, either: ***co-decision procedure*** with Economic and Social Committee ***and Committee of the Regions*** consulted;
- or: Commission proposal — European Parliament, Economic and Social Committee ***and Committee of the Regions*** consulted, — Council acting unanimously.

35. Development cooperation

Measures necessary to further the Community's development cooperation objectives (such as multiannual programmes) (Article 179, ex Article 130 W):

- ***co-decision procedure.***

Negotiation and conclusion of agreements between the Community and third countries or international organisations (Article 181, ex Article 130 Y):

- Article 300 procedure (ex Article 228): Commission recommendations to Council — Council authorises Commission to open and conduct the necessary negotiations in conjunction with the special committees appointed by the Council and in line with directives fixed by the Council — agreement concluded by Council (by qualified majority or unanimously depending on procedure required for the adoption of internal rules).

36. Association of the overseas countries and territories

Establishing provisions on the detailed rules and procedure for the association of the overseas countries and territories of the Community (Article 187, ex Article 136):

- Council acting unanimously.

37. Institutional provisions (list not exhaustive)

Establishing a uniform procedure for elections by direct universal suffrage to the European Parliament (Article 190***(4)***, ex Article 138):

- Council acting unanimously after obtaining assent of European Parliament acting by a majority of its component members — ratification by Member States in accordance with their respective constitutional requirements.

Establishing principles and rules governing executive powers conferred by the Council (Article 202, ex Article 145):

- Commission proposal — European Parliament consulted — Council acting unanimously.

Fixing the order in which the Member States are to hold the Presidency of the Council (Article 203, ***second subparagraph***, ex Article 146):

- Council acting unanimously.

38. Financial provisions (list not exhaustive)

Laying down provisions relating to the system of own resources of the Community (Article 269, ex Article 201):

- Commission proposal — European Parliament consulted Council acting unanimously — ratification by Member States in accordance with their respective constitutional requirements.

Adoption of Community budget (Article 272, ex Article 203):

- Preliminary draft budget submitted to Council by Commission by 1 September — draft budget adopted by Council acting by a qualified majority and placed before European Parliament by 5 October —within 45 days, the European Parliament may amend the draft budget in the case of non-compulsory expenditure or propose modifications in the case of compulsory expenditure — draft budget altered in line with the amendments and modifications accepted or rejected by the Council acting by qualified majority, and then placed before the European Parliament — the European Parliament may, within 15 days and acting by a majority of its Members and three fifths of the votes cast, amend or reject the modifications to its amendments (non-compulsory expenditure) made by the Council and adopt the budget accordingly; alternatively the European Parliament, acting by a majority of its Members and two thirds of the votes cast, may reject the draft budget and ask for a new draft to be submitted to it — the President of the European Parliament declares that the budget has been finally adopted.

Adopting the necessary measures in the fields of the prevention of and fight against fraud affecting the financial interests of the Community with a view to affording effective and equivalent protection in the Member States (without prejudice to the application of national criminal law or the national administration of justice.) (Article 280***(4)***, ex Article 209 A):

- co-decision procedure with Court of Auditors consulted.

39. General and final provisions (list not exhaustive)

Laying down the Staff Regulations of officials of the European Communities and the Conditions of Employment of other servants of those Communities (Article 283, ex Article 212):

- Commission proposal — institutions concerned consulted — Council acting by a qualified majority.

Making changes to the list of products connected with the production of or trade in arms, munitions and war material (Article 296, ex Article 223):

- Commission proposal — Council acting unanimously.

Adoption of special measures fixing the conditions for applying the Treaty establishing the European Community to the outermost regions (Article 299***(2)***, ex Article 227):

- Commission proposal — European Parliament consulted — Council acting by a qualified majority.

Adopting the necessary urgent measures where a common position or a joint action adopted according to the provisions of the Treaty on European Union relating to the common foreign and security policy provides for action to interrupt or to reduce economic relations with one or more third countries (Article 301, ex Article 228 A):

- Commission proposal — Council acting by a qualified majority.

European Commission

The Amsterdam Treaty: A comprehensive guide

Luxembourg: Office for Official Publications of the European Communities

1999 — 96 pp. — 21 x 29.7 cm

ISBN 92–828–7951–8